Liberty *or* Justice for All?

Also by Philip F. Gura

Man's Better Angels: Romantic Reformers and the Coming of the Civil War

The Life of William Apess, Pequot

Truth's Ragged Edge: The Rise of the American Novel

The American Antiquarian Society, 1812–2012: A Bicentennial History

American Transcendentalism: A History

Jonathan Edwards: America's Evangelical

C. F. Martin and His Guitars, 1796–1873

Buried from the World: Inside the Massachusetts State Prison, 1829–1831

America's Instrument: The Banjo in the Nineteenth Century (with James Bollman)

The Crossroads of American History and Literature

A Glimpse of Sion's Glory: Puritan Radicalism in New England, 1620–1660

Critical Essays in American Transcendentalism (with Joel Myerson)

The Wisdom of Words: Language, Theology, and Literature in the New England Renaissance

Liberty *or* Justice for All?

A CONVERSATION ACROSS THE AMERICAN CENTURIES

Philip F. Gura

The University of Georgia Press
Athens

Athens, Georgia 30602
www.ugapress.org

Set in Minion Pro by Melissa Buchanan
Printed and bound by Books International

The paper in this book meets the guidelines for permanence and durability of the Committee on Production Guidelines for Book Longevity of the Council on Library Resources.

Most University of Georgia Press titles are available from popular e-book vendors.

Printed in the United States of America
22 23 24 25 26 P 5 4 3 2 1

Library of Congress Control Number: 2022948284
ISBN: 9780820363127 (hardback)
ISBN: 9780820363110 (paperback)
ISBN: 9780820363103 (ebook)

For David D. Hall

He had an uncommon thirst for knowledge, in the pursuit of which he spared no Cost or Pains. . . . Tho' his Principles were Calvinistic, yet he called no Man, Father. He thought and judged for himself and was truly very much of an Original.

SAMUEL HOPKINS ON JONATHAN EDWARDS (1765)

Contents

Acknowledgments

This book has had a long gestation, for most of its history massaged and polished by Thomas Lebien, who has edited several of my books. I thank him for having confidence in the importance of writing about this group of thinkers, particularly at this stage of our nation's history.

I also note my indebtedness to those scholars who most recently have themselves stressed the significance of Edwards, Emerson, James, and Rawls, particularly the late Robert D. Richardson Jr., whose conversation and scholarship long has been an inspiration. And the same with this volume's dedicatee, David D. Hall, each of whose many works exemplifies the nature of dedicated and uncompromising scholarship, inoculated as it is against the latest academic fever.

Finally, I have much appreciated the continuing support of the Department of English and Comparative Literature at the University of North Carolina at Chapel Hill and particularly of its most recent chair, Mary Floyd-Wilson, who always has appreciated and expedited my work.

Acknowledgments

Liberty *or* Justice for All?

Introduction

This book focuses on four thinkers—the theologian Jonathan Edwards, the author Ralph Waldo Emerson, the psychologist William James, and the moral philosopher John Rawls—who indelibly marked American history through their publication of large-scale theoretical works that offer blueprints for the realization of a just society. In particular, their works illustrate the nation's struggles to guarantee a modicum of freedom for each individual, as well as of justice for all of its citizens.

Many others—Thomas Jefferson, Margaret Fuller, Frederick Douglass, Elizabeth Cady Stanton, and W. E. B. Du Bois, to name but a few of the most obvious—also spoke to this issue but not with both the immediate and lasting effects of the above quartet's works. With their focus on the creation of a free and just society, these individuals, though separated in time, seem almost in imaginary conversation with each other.

My purpose is to follow a prominent thread in an elaborate braided fabric, from the early eighteenth century to the late twentieth century. As this thread was woven through the emerging American tapestry, four concerns, often in conflict, gave it texture: God, self, community, and the state. How these four concepts connect or intersect composes a distinct and gripping narrative of people, places, and ideas. The arc of this history moves from the presence and then gradual receding of an imminent God; to a reliance first on the individual, then on democratic community; and finally, in the twentieth century, on the accelerating growth of an ever more present and intrusive state. The chief question becomes, if once America was conceived as "one nation under God," how did it change as its citizens learned that belief in both the divine and the divinely inspired individual was becoming less and less determinative in their lives, superseded by the nation-state?

If every American is guaranteed life, liberty, and the pursuit of happiness, should this be a nation where the individual reigns supreme? Or, if all people are created equal, is it one in which everyone should always look out for the other? In the Pledge of Allegiance, a version of which was first formulated during the Civil War but did not reach its final form until 1954, Americans speak of a nation "with liberty and justice for all," but when has this ever been more than an unrealized ideal?

Historians have often described this choice between self or society as that between classical liberalism, which champions the rights of individuals in a laissez-faire, market economy, or civic republicanism, with its emphasis on placing the good of the commonwealth ahead of personal interest. At least since Alexander Hamilton, James Madison, and John Jay's heroic attempt in the *Federalist Papers* (1788), the nation has attempted to hold these opposing value systems in delicate balance, trying to realize the promise of both liberty *and* justice for all (and in the mid-twentieth-century's version, even adding, as though trying to return to its earliest incarnation, that it was "one nation *under God*"). But when things go awry—as, say, in the constitutional scrum following the Declaration of Independence; in the 1850s, when slavery threatened national cataclysm; in the 1890s, when eastern European immigrants flooded in, challenging their neighbors with strange religions and folkways; in the 1960s, when battles over civil rights and the Vietnam War rocked the nation from coast to coast; or again in 2016, when the presidential race divided the nation as it had not been since the Civil War—how would Americans accommodate the necessary redefinition of their national ideals?

Over three centuries, there evolved certain habits of thought used to address and resolve such conflicts. But even today the questions remain. Is it self or society that demands one's allegiance? What are individuals' obligations to their communities or to the state, and what does the state owe them? Most citizens, for example, pay taxes for local schools even when they have no students in them; but do they evince the same generosity when immigrants displaced by war need the basic necessities of life in their new homes? Should the rich be taxed at a higher rate to create new jobs for the poor in the ghettoized urban environment? How far do the rights of private ownership extend when one's land is needed for the completion of a new interstate highway? Just which individual rights should a society guarantee, and what kinds of behavior should it encourage? And, as the United States moved from a concern with what people owed God to what citizens owed each other and themselves, what was religion's role in an increasingly secularized, pluralistic state? At least since the seventeenth century, when English Puritans sought to create in the Massachusetts Bay Colony a New Jerusalem based on an ethic of Christian charity, Americans have sought to resolve the conflicts and contradictions arising from answers to such questions. How they have done so comprises an important part of America's intellectual and cultural legacy. As we still grapple with them, we can do worse than reconsider four thinkers who understood what was at stake in their resolution.

Jonathan Edwards was a New England clergyman praised in Europe as well as British North America as one of the eighteenth century's great minds. He was a product and supporter of extensive religious revivals that swept the continent from Nova Scotia to Georgia, championing a starkly Calvinist worldview, and worshipping an incomprehensible and omnipotent deity who controlled the work of redemption, even as Edwards encouraged hope for a renewed Christian community based in Gospel charity.

Beginning in the 1730s from his pulpit in Northampton, Massachusetts, later as a missionary to Native Americans along the frontier, and then as president of the College of New Jersey (later Princeton), Edwards encouraged, explained, and defended the Great Awakening.

He even wondered if the recent revivals signaled the beginning of the Millennium, the prophesied thousand years of peace and joy that would precede Christ's triumphant return.[1]

To hasten efforts toward that glorious time, Edwards promulgated a social ethic based in universal love, regardless of gender, class, or race, for he believed that God's saving grace knew no such distinctions. In 1746, in his *Treatise Concerning the Religious Affections*, he outlined twelve signs of truly religious "affections" or emotions and considered the most important those that "have their exercise and fruit in Christian practice." Some twenty years later, in his *Nature of True Virtue*, a text that English political philosopher and novelist William Godwin later cited admiringly in his *Enquiry Concerning Political Justice*, Edwards went even further.[2] He declared that true virtue most essentially consists in "benevolence to being in general," that is, in love to *all* of God's creation. Through the Second Great Awakening in the early nineteenth century to the Civil War, his theology remained the starting point for serious debates about peoples' relation to God and both their and God's relations to civil society.

Edwards's ideas did not go unchallenged. In attempting to make his ideas more accessible, some of his disciples diluted the grand vision that he articulated, the better to meet the challenge from, and so to align it with, emergent utilitarianism. As early as the Revolutionary period, some began to measure virtue not as part of the distant logic of the Gospel plan but, as Benjamin Franklin put it in his *Autobiography*, by "the nature of man alone considered."[3] From here, it was a small step to the proposition that the general welfare should be considered not as the greatest *good* as *God intends it* but as the greatest happiness of the greatest number of people *as one understands it*. As the founders of the nation grappled with the proper balance of liberalism and civic republicanism to attain this goal, the pendulum swung back and forth, particularly through the influence of such utilitarian philosophers as Francis Hutcheson and Jeremy Bentham on James Madison and other of the Founding Fathers, and John Stuart Mill's on the subsequent generation.

But even if Franklin's and Jefferson's deism pushed them to view the world as increasingly man- (and woman-) centered, the United States as a whole remained Christian. The new emphasis on each individual's free will meant different things to different individuals for whom the spiritual life remained a vivid reality, be their faith conservative or liberal. To a Free Will Baptist or Methodist, for example, it engendered the thought that human effort itself was efficacious for one's salvation; while, to others, the Calvinists' (like Edwards's) emphasis on God's sovereign grace remained the only way to salvation.

Nowhere was this shift to the inherent worth—even the divinity—of the individual more visible than in the career and writings of Ralph Waldo Emerson, a liberal Christian—he began in the Unitarian ministry—who by the end of the Civil War had been anointed the country's representative philosopher. Writing a century after Edwards but aware and appreciative of his works—one of Emerson's friends recalled that he was fond of acknowledging his spiritual affinity to Edwards—Emerson followed his father into Unitarianism, a liberal Protestant denomination with its center in the Northeast. (One wit termed it the brotherhood of man, under the Fatherhood of God, in the neighborhood of Boston!) Soon enough, however, Emerson realized that his faith too often lacked an affective, spiritual dimension. It was, he complained, "corpse-cold." He began to read widely in English and European Romanticism, and by the mid-1830s grafted onto his liberal Christianity an empowering belief in each individual's innate divinity.

When one understood that "the currents of the universal being" flowed through one and made one (as Emerson put it in his seminal book *Nature*) "part or particle of God," one gained an inerrant moral compass. The deepest knowledge of spiritual reality is thus congenial to the mind of each individual. This proposition informed what became known as New England transcendentalism, a constellation of ideas that defined the nation's first bona fide intellectual coterie, with among its members abolitionist Theodore Parker, feminist Margaret

Fuller, champion of the laboring classes Orestes Brownson, and early environmentalist Henry David Thoreau.

Unlike Edwards, who held that only some people were among God's elect, Emerson proclaimed that the transformative religious experience that marked one's election was an integral part of humanity's moral constitution and so available to all. By his reading, the Gospels announced that every person is a son or daughter of God, connected to the "Oversoul." And when one lives from the spirit—directs one's behavior in accordance with conscience or intuition—one becomes truly self-reliant, a proposition that dovetailed with the political principles of the nation's young democracy and is typified in Emerson's most well-known essay, "Self-Reliance."

In a period of transformative changes in notions of space and time that accompanied such inventions as the railroad, the telegraph, the steamboat, photography, as well as industrialization as a whole, Emerson's essay struck a nerve. The awakened and transformed individual would innately know how to respond to these changes and how to go forward confidently as a citizen in the new nation, true both to him- or herself, as well as to the citizenry as a whole, the least of whom were as divine as she or he.

Edwards's conception of the good society was based in social cooperation and cemented with love, but he doubted that such cooperation alone could improve people because it might sap what rapidly was becoming one's treasured individuality. The less government we have the better, he proclaimed in his essay "Politics." The antidote to the widespread social dissonance was the cultivation of private character in ways that then would spill over into good citizenship. If government did not encourage self-culture as its main goal, it would become corrupt, beholden primarily to property interests rather than to the country's population as a whole.

The more one lived by conscience, Emerson believed, the less government would be necessary, a belief echoed by his friend and onetime disciple Henry David Thoreau in his now-famous essay on civil disobedience: "There will never be," he wrote, "a really free and enlightened State, until the State comes to recognize the individual as a higher and independent power, from which all its own power and authority are derived, and treats him accordingly."[4]

Beginning in the 1840s, however, when Emerson gave a celebrated antislavery address in his hometown of Concord, Massachusetts, he realized that in the general populace there was not strict nor widespread enough reliance on the moral sentiment to attain justice without some sort of artificial restraints on rampant self-centeredness, what Edwards understood as the most visible mark of humanity's sinfulness. Unfortunately, conscience alone would not end the southerners' devotion to and defense of slavery, nor the northern Cotton Whigs' toleration of a southern economy whose chief product—cotton—they desperately needed. It took internecine warfare to destroy the horror of chattel slavery.

As Abraham Lincoln knew, the Civil War demanded unprecedented sacrifice for and unquestioning allegiance to the commonwealth, now defined as the Union. Emerson's once self-sufficient and triumphant individual became only a tiny cog in a vast war machine. This diminution of what he once celebrated as an imperial self only accelerated after 1865 as the nation scrambled to recover from the war's devastating consequences, for reconstruction of the Union was unfeasible without large-scale industrialization as well as federal intervention.

Even through these dark years, though, many Americans were loath to abandon Emerson's promise that all was possible for those who strived for self-improvement. Impatient with his more abstruse philosophical principles, they simplified some of his ideas and simply ignored others. They applied his thought more to the material than to the spiritual realm and aligned it with the demands of the market economy. There his acolytes became less self-reliant individuals than champions of laissez-faire capitalism and participants in the rough-and-tumble of the increasingly divisive two-party political system. Many people twisted and turned his words, isolating single sentences from their complex context to support a myth of the American as a self-made individual who "hitch[ed his] wagon to a star" for his betterment, now more and more often defined, as it had been for Franklin, as economic success. Steel magnate Andrew Carnegie put it this way: "Aim for the highest . . . for, as Emerson says, 'no one can cheat you out of ultimate success but yourselves.'"[5]

But proud of Emerson's ever-growing international reputation and ignoring the larger implications of his vision, Americans touted him as a national institution, the veritable "sage of Concord." They crowned him as the philosopher king of rugged individualism who counseled Americans to prevail, against all odds, particularly where their self-interest was concerned.

Eventually, Emerson's idealism, tempered as it was by his growing sense that ethical engagement itself was the only means of spiritual fulfillment, became increasingly out of step in a world influenced less by the hand of God than by Darwin's theory of natural selection, now applied to the social realm by sociologists Herbert Spencer and William Graham Sumner. In the late nineteenth century, visions of a just society based in love for perfectly equal, individual souls persisted here and there—among champions of cooperative ownership of factories, say; or proponents of a "Social Gospel" who sought to apply New Testament principles to the nation's manifold social problems; or in utopian fiction like reformer Edward Bellamy's immensely popular *Looking Backward, 2000–1887* (1888) and feminist Charlotte Perkins Gilman's *Herland* (1915). But these efforts alone could not stay the "robber barons" who dominated what Mark Twain and Charles Dudley Warner aptly dubbed the Gilded Age, rooted firmly in continued dilution of the nation's once divinely ordained purpose as well as in diminution of the power and significance of the individual.

To understand and accommodate this brave new world from which God seemed gradually withdrawing if not was wholly absent, William James brought to bear ideas both from Edwards, whom he cited approvingly as a master psychologist of religious experience, and from his literal godfather, Emerson. James resituated Edwards's Calvinism and Emerson's transcendentalism within a new set of philosophical and psychological principles—grounded in "pragmatism" and "radical empiricism" (the belief that knowledge flows exclusively from experience)—and transformed how Americans understood individual and social responsibility, through acceptance and encouragement of pluralistic community.

From his father, a disciple of the Swedish mystic Emanuel Swedenborg and the French socialist Charles Fourier, James inherited the belief that selfishness is the cardinal sin and, conversely, that man reaches his "redeemed" state not in isolation but only in society. James also treasured the "cash-value" or usefulness of each person's experience, spiritual or otherwise, and heartily embraced Darwin's understanding that life consists of constant change or motion, an idea that Emerson had anticipated in his essay "Experience."

Like Emerson, too, James understood that the miraculous lies in the common, so that at each moment, through even the most seemingly insignificant actions, each individual makes truth and value anew. For James, willingness to take up any challenge the universe presented, to treat any test as if, at that moment, it matters most, is what makes a life significant. Good citizenship depended on such considered action for the *demos*, the people as a whole, regardless of personal beliefs about God or nature.

In the first years of the twentieth century, James's propositions about the relativity of truth and his embrace of an open-ended, ever-evolving universe resonated among Americans who increasingly viewed spirituality as only one of many ways of knowing and being in the world. Many in the new generation dismissed organized religion as an impediment to self-understanding as well as social improvement. They began to endorse large-scale governmental intervention to remedy the increasing problems initiated by unprecedented immigration, the formation of immense industrial monopolies, and inhumane working conditions for the laboring classes, all of which worked against the inclusive, humanistic community that James championed. This was the era of the "muckrakers," like Lincoln Steffens, Jacob Riis, and Ida

Tarbell, who urged the government to break industrial monopolies, indict corrupt officeholders, set reasonable working conditions for the laborer, grant women suffrage, and regulate banking for the good of all citizens.

James's signature ideas meshed with such contemporary social experiments as the settlement house movement (epitomized by Jane Addams's Hull House) and John Dewey's reconfiguration of democratic education, as well as with a Progressive movement whose emphasis was on modernization in all arenas—industry, science, politics, and society. But even as James had one foot in this new secular world, he continued to defend the pragmatic value of religious faith ahead of the cataclysm of the First World War, which forever changed the terms of belief.

After the horror of that worldwide conflagration, many Americans no longer believed in a universe ruled by a benevolent deity nor manageable by either the individual efforts of Emerson's transcendent individuals or the confluence of James's democratically enlightened people. Instead, these participants in the Modernist movement turned to such new fields of inquiry as physics, psychoanalysis, and sociology to understand the world. As James counseled, each person made his or her own truth, based in experience, but crucially, also tolerated others' opinions for the betterment and preservation of democratic community. In the 1930s, when an untethered individualist ethos again wrought havoc in the economic realm and brought the nation to social and political paralysis, James's emphasis on active process and pragmatic result remained efficacious, most notably in President Franklin D. Roosevelt's efforts to right the listing ship of state with his New Deal.

But while the safety nets established during the 1930s slowly brought a degree of social stability, through the remainder of the century arguments persisted about the need for and function of governmental entitlement programs such as Social Security and, later, Medicare,

Medicaid, the War on Poverty, and the Affordable Care Act. With the two major political parties aligned on opposite sides, Democrats supporting entitlements that "big" government guaranteed and Republicans urging less governmental intrusion into individuals' lives and questioning the putative worth of federal "handouts," the twentieth century's preeminent moral philosopher, John Rawls, offered his influential *Theory of Justice.*

Although raised in a strongly Christian family, Rawls came to reject religion as an organizing principle of a truly just society. Rather, he believed that secular, pluralistic democracy has to rest on a foundation of justice—"justice as fairness," he termed it—to which all citizens, regardless of their differences and disagreements, could pledge allegiance. To his mind, a truly democratic polity grew from social institutions such as an agreed upon constitution and laws (particularly those concerning property), as well as on sound economic policy, universal education, and universal health care. The goal was to establish fair and inclusive rules that provided a framework for cooperation to provide for all of the citizenry's essential needs.

The link to James is clear: Rawls sought to understand on what ideas a pluralistic society might agree and how these would reinforce a nation's core values and institutions. Gone, now, was any mention of the guiding power of religion, the supreme power of the individual, or the restorative power of democratic pragmatism. Rather than reform policy to eliminate inequality in any one constituency singled out for assistance, as, say, in Lyndon Johnson's War on Poverty, Rawls focused on a "reasonable pluralism" based in an identification of how people, despite holding different religious and philosophical views, might exist harmoniously, as long as they agreed on the moral foundation of their society.

Against his chief bogey, the utilitarianism of Jeremy Bentham and his Enlightenment peers, and then of John Stuart Mill, whose advocates sought to maximize the *average* level of happiness in society, Rawls urged the rearrangement of social institutions to guarantee *everyone's* well-being. This constitutes the basis of free society, he argued, and any attempts to eradicate injustice—specific matters that divide a polity on which people might disagree—inevitably end in unfairness and, potentially, oppression. In a truly pluralistic world, the state cannot rest on any strictly enforced, singular worldview, whether promulgated by church or state, but on that which, given peoples' diversity of views and circumstances, any of them could agree as essential to a harmonious society.

Rawls's is not a religious or philosophical conception of justice. It is a *political* one based in consensus among widely different parties. In contemporary society, just as diversity exists, so should general toleration. As the divine receded like an outgoing tide and as the harsh realities of the twentieth century shattered both the power of the individual and the idea of a privileged community (think of Hiroshima and Auschwitz, the Tulsa Race Massacre and Wounded Knee), an expanded role for the state became necessary.

Separated in time as they are, these four thinkers promulgated what on the surface may seem like different notions of selfhood, citizenship, community, and state. But because of their ideas' very universality, they should continue to inform discussions of the religious, political, and social bases of democratic institutions, the obligations they entail, and the commonwealth they define and support. These thinkers demonstrate how otherwise rarefied ideas, as they work out themselves in the political arena, become instruments wielded on behalf of particular interests, or articulations, if sometimes vulgarized, of certain material conditions.

The responsibilities of individuals and communities, each to the other, are ever present in these thinkers' writings, as are the potentially intrusive powers of God or government. It was not the case then, or now, that Edwards should be absent from our repertoire of ideas and convictions, nor should Emerson or James. Similarly, Rawls, who died in 2002 and already has been followed by two generations of thinkers, both critics and defenders, offered ideas as relevant as they ever were in the 1970s. The braiding of these thinkers' threads continues, some strengthening and some fraying in the warp of history and the inscrutability of fate. Their guiding propositions endure: the relationship of individuals to God as well as to community, and the mutual obligations of citizens to state. Although separated temporally, these thinkers centered their ideas on the balance between individual sovereignty and communal responsibility in a Christian nation, a problem that has haunted and befuddled the United States since its foundation and confounds it still.

At different times and in different situations, many Americans have praised the texts of Edwards, Emerson, James, and Rawls as indicative of how one might realize an equitable democratic polity. The first three tackled the seemingly intractable problem of how European settlers in the New World and, later, citizens of the United States could strike a balance between God, self, and other, and thus realize the destiny to which Americans believed they were called. The fourth sought to craft a model for a moral society in a universe from which God was now not present, if not permanently absent, and in which the nation-state now was the norm, though ever under challenge by people of different tribes, religions, or politics.

Americans have routinely returned to the leading lights of their political history—Madison and Hamilton, Lincoln and Franklin Roosevelt, Du Bois and Martin Luther King Jr.—for inspiration and practical guidance. But wrestling at length with the unresolvable; delineating the fault lines of our convictions and our commitments; and articulating the ideas and ideals that are the building blocks of our perpetually incomplete pursuit of a more perfect union, Edwards, Emerson, James, and Rawls shed revealing light on where we have come from and, consequently, whither our errand may yet take us. These four thinkers continue to deserve sustained attention, for while their ideas do not necessarily align in one grand design, each continues to offer wisdom that, when strengthened or tempered by observations and recommendations of other seminal thinkers, helps us to conceive a nation that provides liberty *and* justice for all.

1
Jonathan Edwards

HEAVEN IS A WORLD OF LOVE

A Guest at the Door

In the late autumn of 1742, Charles Chauncy, minister of Boston's First Church, was in a funk. During the hot, humid months of summer he had made a three-hundred-mile circuit, from New Hampshire to New Jersey, visiting clergymen and Harvard College classmates to glean details about the extensive religious revivals spreading like wildfire and reconfiguring the colonies' social landscape. To that same end, with other friends and acquaintances he had carried on an extensive correspondence, exchanging hundreds of letters about the disruptions to public order that issued from the revivals. This work left him debilitated, and after his exhausting travels he spent several months recuperating from what became a chronic condition—a "colick," he termed it.[1]

That same summer the religious excitement that so preoccupied Chauncy literally came to his door when the young Reverend James Davenport, an ardent supporter of "the great and general awakenings," paid him a visit.[2] A recent Yale College graduate, Davenport had been inspired by the English preacher George Whitefield, who had come to the colonies in 1739 and had fanned the flames of revival from Georgia to Massachusetts. Slender and handsome (and cross-eyed), Whitefield was so effective a preacher that he was called "the Divine Dramatist" and compared to the great English actor David Garrick.[3] On one memorable occasion in Boston, with no church large enough to hold all those eager to hear him, Whitefield moved the service to the Boston Common and addressed a rapt audience of *eight thousand*. Even such a committed skeptic as Benjamin Franklin, who on a lark went to hear Whitefield preach in Philadelphia, emptied his purse when the offering came.

Davenport became one of Whitefield's chief acolytes, and he traveled through New England with "the grand itinerant." Soon, the young minister struck out on his own and became notorious for disrupting church meetings with his histrionic preaching and public castigations of ministers who opposed the revivals. In 1741, in Hartford, Connecticut, he was convicted of violating colony laws against itinerant preaching. The court found him so under the influence "of enthusiastical impressions and impulses, and therefore disturbed in the rational faculties of his mind," that they banished him from the colony.[4] He retreated to his home at Southold on Long Island but soon returned to the road, this time to Boston, where the region's ministerial association, then meeting, had tired of his disruptions and voted to close their pulpits to him. Not cowed, Davenport preached around Boston to whomever would hear him. Finally, he was hauled before the General Court's grand jury for proclaiming that most of the city's ministers were leading their people blindfolded to hell. He received a verdict of non compos mentis and again was remanded to Long Island.

But not before he visited Chauncy, one of the most vociferous critics of Whitefield and his followers. Davenport's was not a courtesy call: he had come to interrogate Chauncy about the state of his soul. Was the First Church's minister truly a man of God, Davenport wanted to know, or like so many of his colleagues, a hypocrite who demanded deference to settled clergy, even if they were "unconverted"? Was Chauncy "Brother" or "Neighbor," he bluntly asked. In other words, was he one of Davenport's party who supported the revivals or just another backsliding colonist?

Chauncy refused to answer the question. Instead, he excoriated his visitor. Davenport's behavior, Chauncy told him, had nothing to do with true religion but only encouraged his followers to think of it as "a wild, disorderly, imaginary business." He condemned Davenport's impertinence in thinking that he could judge another man's soul, something reserved to God alone. "If ever GOD gives you *a sound mind*,"

Chauncy told him, "you will *cry to him from the deeps*, for this strange conduct you have unhappily fallen into." Showing Davenport to the door, he chastised him for taking the "*notions of your own mind*, for *divine communications*."[5]

Chauncy knew that his impertinent visitor represented only the tip of the iceberg, for as soon as Davenport left the area, other radical New Lights, as the revivalists were called, took his place, threatening the region's hierarchical order as they unsettled congregation after congregation. More problematic, however, was Jonathan Edwards, a Northampton, Massachusetts, minister who, though more moderate, had become the revivals' chief defender and interpreter.

Edwards had assumed this position in part through publication of his *Faithful Narrative of the Surprising Work of God* (1737), an account of a series of revivals that he had initiated in 1735 in the Connecticut River Valley. Highly successful as an evangelist, he welcomed Whitefield and other itinerants and sincerely believed that the current religious upheaval was the work of God. But Chauncy thought Edwards, for all his intelligence, as deluded as Whitefield and Davenport. Given Chauncy's stature among the colony's Old Lights, it fell to him to rebut Edwards's defense of the awakenings.

The Edwards-Chauncy debates had profound political ramifications. What alarmed both men, though in different ways, was the tattered state of his contemporaries' affairs. Edwards saw an increasingly divided society less driven by a desire to improve the state of their souls than to aggrandize themselves in an emergent market economy. The result was increasing social fluidity dependent on the ownership of land, livestock, and other marketable goods. For Edwards, one's relationship to God and the Holy Spirit was the most important consideration; but for many others, status within a community now trumped religious duties and influenced local and provincial politics. Edwards wanted to reorder priorities so that personal religion once again had precedence, so that one might live *in* the world but not be *of* it. Only then could there be social harmony.

Chauncy felt differently. He had not crisscrossed New England just to assess the dangers of a market economy or to gauge the direction of the political winds. He, too, truly wanted to learn about the state of the colonists' souls and their churches, but to him most problematic were the ways in which the prorevival cohort challenged traditional rules of order and deference. Preachers without college educations, laypeople challenging clerical authority, congregations splitting apart over points of doctrine—these attacks in an increasingly volatile social order threatened him and other conservative clergy who saw in the revivals nothing but social turmoil and in the young Edwards the revivals' most sophisticated defender.

The Young Evangelist

Jonathan Edwards was born in 1703 (the same year as Chauncy) in East Windsor, Connecticut, to Timothy and Esther Edwards, the sixth child in a family of, eventually, eleven, including ten girls.[6] His father had graduated from Harvard College in 1691 (with a joint AB and MA), and three years later the East Windsor church called him to their pastorate. The same year that Timothy assumed the pulpit, he married Esther Stoddard, the daughter of Solomon Stoddard, minister to Northampton, Massachusetts, and the most respected and venerated clergyman in the Connecticut River Valley.

The young Edwards prepared for college with his father and at the age of thirteen joined ten other boys at the Collegiate School of Connecticut (after 1718, Yale College), founded in 1701 to offset Harvard's accelerating drift from Calvinistic doctrine. After a short stint preaching in New York City, he returned to Yale and received his MA. Another brief pastorate, in nearby Bolton, Connecticut, followed, and then Edwards again returned to Yale, where he remained for two more years as a tutor.

While at Yale he met fifteen-year-old Sarah Pierpont. His infatuation was immediate. She was "beloved of that great Being who made and rules the world," he noted in a private journal entry, who at certain times "comes to her and fills her mind with exceeding delight." Sarah was "of a wonderful sweetness, calmness, and universal benevolence of mind," he continued, and loved to be alone "walking in the fields and groves, and seems always to have someone invisible conversing with her."[7] Both smitten, they soon were engaged. Around the same time, Northampton sought someone to assist the aging Stoddard. Edwards seemed an ideal candidate. Early in 1727 he was ordained, and that summer he and Sarah, now seventeen, married.

Sadly, Edwards did not benefit for long from Stoddard's counsel. Early in 1729 the great man died, after almost sixty years in the ministry. Edwards earnestly sought to be worthy of his grandfather's mantle. Tall and slender, about six feet, and delicately featured—one biographer spoke of him as "of a feminine cast"—he had "a broad, bold forehead, and an eye unusually piercing and luminous."[8] By all accounts, the young minister's work ethic was prodigious. He typically spent thirteen hours a day in his study, punctuating his labors with recreation, usually walking, riding, or if the snow was too deep, chopping wood. In warmer seasons, he regularly rode two or three miles to some lonely grove where he would dismount and walk for a while, jotting thoughts on small pieces of paper that he pinned to his clothes for the ride back. He kept morning and evening prayers with his family and daily instructed his children in the Bible.

Edwards's pulpit manner reflected his rather reserved constitution. Unlike the preaching of so many New Lights, his was not overly emotional. His delivery was natural, his voice not particularly loud. But he appeared in the pulpit with such gravity and spoke with such distinctness, clearness, and precision, that he commanded his audience. By the early 1730s he had found his chief topic, the "great salvation revealed in the Gospel." Focusing on God's sovereignty, man's utter depravity, and the excellence of Christ, he devoted himself to awakening his flock to their true spiritual condition. Other clergy in the valley joined him in his promulgation of orthodox Calvinism, but the key in which he delivered his message set him off from his cohort and contributed to his remarkable success as a preacher.

Souls Flying to Christ

Edwards saw God's free grace as a divine illumination that irresistibly and irrevocably transformed a person's experience of spiritual matters, a change that he memorably described in a 1733 sermon, "A Divine and Supernatural Light." When one is converted, he argued, God immediately imparts a spiritual light to the soul that is of "a different nature from any that is obtained by natural means." God acts in the minds of the elect, he explained, "as an indwelling vital principle" that gives "a due apprehension" of the Gospel. The renovated person has a different "sense of the heart," accompanied by "a sense of the beauty, amiableness, and sweetness" of the Christian truths. A divine and supernatural light thus fills the heart and changes its nature, effectually disposing one to a "universal holiness of life" that he or she demonstrates in all dealings with family, neighbors, and community.[9] Such was the lesson that Edwards delivered to his flock week after week and that he hoped would animate them to live in Christian harmony.

Late in 1734 he saw positive results. In sermons aimed specifically at young people who were increasingly taken to frivolity and "frolicking," he warned of life's utter fragility and prayed for regenerated hearts to correct such disruptive behavior. He brought to mind recent tragedies, such as the plight of a young man who had been violently seized with pleurisy (an inflammation of the lungs), become delirious, and died two days later. His sudden death shocked the young people, whose concern was heightened when a short time later a young woman also passed. Before her final illness, she worried about her salvation, but deeply moved by Edwards's sermons, she was able to die "full of comfort," even as she implored others to heed his council. These two events "solemnized" the minds of Northampton's young people. At Edwards's suggestion they began to spend some of their evenings in "social religion," dividing themselves into groups that met in different parts of the town to discuss the points of doctrine that they had heard from the pulpit.[10]

But not only young people needed reformation. Distressed by the jealousy and acrimony over land distribution and the accompanying bickering over social status that was tearing apart the community, Edwards also sought to awaken the adult population. With each passing week his words proved more effective. This general community awakening proved to him that he truly was witnessing the Lord's work. Then, in late December 1735 the dam burst as the spirit of God set in "extraordinarily." The excitement began with the conversions of five or six people, one a woman who had been one of the greatest "company-keepers"—that is, profligate and probably dissipated. When word spread that God had given her a new heart, "truly broken and sanctified," the news affected people throughout the town. Many sought out the convert, and her words greatly touched even those who had never shown any serious interest in religion.

Remarkably, in a community that was the shire town, as well as the chief market center of the region, people began to neglect all but the most necessary tasks, preferring instead to spend their time in religious exercises. They put aside the petty backbiting that for years had marked the town, where there had long prevailed a "spirit of contention" between two parties—social classes, really—into which Northampton had for many years been divided. The town never had been so "full of love, nor so full of joy," Edwards wrote.[11] All meetings, religious and secular, were imbued with the community's renewed embrace of Christian charity. It seemed the heaven on earth for which Edwards long had prayed.

Subsequently, many visitors to the town (whether they were there to see family, were on business, or had been drawn from curiosity about the revival) were similarly wrought upon. When they carried news back home of the remarkable events they had witnessed, revivals broke out among their brethren, too, further fueling the belief that this work was extraordinary. When Edwards later quantified the results of these awakenings, he counted no fewer than thirty-two communities up and down the Connecticut River, from Northfield, in Massachusetts, to New Haven and Groton in Connecticut, that had been awakened. The New England colonies had never seen anything like it.

Some, however, doubted that the events were anything more than the result of rampant self-deception or copycat behavior. One unsympathetic Anglican clergyman found the converts' behavior particularly unsettling. "Sadness and horror seize them, and hold them some days," he wrote. Eventually, some feel an inward joy that often first showed itself in such incongruous behavior as "laughing in the meeting," while others were "sad for want of experiencing this work." Everywhere, he wrote, "[t]he canting question trumped about is, *are you gone through*? i.e. Conversion."[12]

Others soon joined the Reverend Timothy Cutler, an Anglican, in refusing to acknowledge any positive effects from the revivals, even as Edwards countered that the positive results were undeniable. More and more people presented themselves at the bimonthly communion services. During the six months of the revival, Edwards calculated that more than three hundred were "savingly brought home to Christ." Equally significant, the new church members were of all ages, not just the youth whose conversions had initiated the revival. From his pulpit, Edwards saw ample evidence that this great work was bearing fruit. He redoubled his efforts.

Then trouble started. Some individuals who eagerly wished that they were regenerated, but who "continue[d] wandering in such a kind of labyrinth ten times as long as others," fell into despair. The devil found his opening: just as the work seemed to peak, "Satan seemed to be more let loose, and raged in a dreadful manner," prompting widespread melancholy. Tragically, Edwards's uncle Joseph Hawley, depressed because he had not been among the awakened, slashed his throat.[13] In a sermon preached shortly after this horrible suicide, Edwards wondered if God had rebuked the town for its heightened spiritual pride. It was time to assess the events, and Chauncy's sharp attacks gave Edwards his opportunity.

Chauncy versus Edwards

Chauncy attacked the first Sunday after Harvard College's commencement in July 1742, when he preached *Enthusiasm Described and Cau-*

tion'd Against. No doubt remembering the wild-eyed Davenport at his door, he argued that an "*Enthusiast*" is someone who thinks of himself as "a person favoured with the extraordinary presence of the Deity" but who mistakes the workings of his own imagination for divine communication. Such a deluded person fancies himself immediately inspired by the spirit of God, when in fact he or she is under no other influence than that of "an over-heated imagination." An enthusiast quite simply has a kind of disease, Chauncy continued, "a sort of madness" that makes him or her disregard "the Dictates of reason."[14]

A hundred miles west, Edwards begged to differ. He acknowledged the damage that Davenport and other radical New Lights had inflicted on his cause, yet he insisted that the visits from English revivalist George Whitefield and other itinerant evangelists reinforced his belief that the revivals were genuine. At Yale College's commencement in 1742 he spoke on *The Distinguishing Marks of a Work of the Spirit*, in which he drew the battle lines. Chauncy had declared that "the plain Truth is, an enlightened Mind, not raised Affections, ought always to be the Guide of those who call themselves Men." But Edwards countered, "If the great things of religion are understood, they must affect the heart."[15] He directed the aspirations of individuals toward a world united in Christian charity. Chauncy tacked in the opposite direction, defending the status quo, particularly the leadership role of an educated ministry, against an increasingly threatened social order in which deference and moderation to the established clergy were thrown aside.

Edwards also issued a still more ambitious and exhaustive defense of religious revival. *Some Thoughts Concerning the Present Revival of Religion in New England*, a 378-page treatise, appeared in late March 1742. Within a year Chauncy, mining his lengthy correspondence and notes, offered his equally extensive *Seasonable Thoughts on the State of Religion in New-England*, whose title and table of contents mirrored Edwards's. "Is it not the great Question of the Day," Chauncy asked rhetorically, "how far, and in what Respects, the Work, going on in the Lands, is the Work of GOD?"[16]

Edwards took pains to distinguish the fruits of the revivals from some of their admittedly deleterious side effects. Because some people were carried away with false impressions and, as a result, were too censorious in their zeal, he acknowledged that the revivals might be attended with errors and downright sinfulness. However, such indications of man's fallen state did not negate the awakening's undeniably positive effects. Chief among these, he explained, was that many of the converted had experienced a divine and supernatural light. This resulted in an irrevocable alteration in the apprehensions, dispositions, and behavior of men that, when replicated in thousands upon thousands, was transforming the colonies (or so Edwards thought) into one harmonious community in which Christian charity reigned.

What precisely were such alterations in personal behavior? First, people became convinced of the truth of the Gospel and through it were led to Christ. Second, they rejected and fought vigorously against Satan's plans to undermine religion. Third, they came to love scripture more than they had before and so were led to a better understanding of their relation to God. Fourth, regeneration engendered in them a spirit of love toward God and man. Because there was abundant evidence of such transformation among so many people as well as newfound harmony in many awakened towns, Edwards could not but conclude that the revivals were God's work.

A few years earlier he had preached a series of sermons (subsequently published) on *The History of Redemption* in which he traced the growth of the Church through recorded time. Now, he placed the recent revivals within this larger frame. It was very likely, he wrote, that the work of God's Spirit was "the dawning, or at least a prelude, to that glorious work of God so often foretold in Scripture, which in the progress and issue of it, shall renew the world of mankind"—that is, that the revivals might presage the prophesied Millennium.[17] Indeed, he boldly proffered, there were many things that made it probable that this work had already begun.

Noting the spread of enthusiastic religion in parts of Europe as well as in the New World, Edwards reminded people of their own recent experiences. It would be ungrateful for them not to take notice, he reminded his congregation, of the "remarkable pouring out of the Spirit of God" that this region of New England recently had experienced and "of which we in this town have had such a share."[18] Edwards was suggesting nothing less than that the long-awaited thousand-year reign of Christ might have begun in Northampton during the "Little Awakening" and now was continuing.

In *Seasonable Thoughts*, Chauncy answered Edwards's arguments point for point, for more was at stake than mere theological grandstanding. Edwards's apocalyptical speculations, which Chauncy regarded as hubristic if not downright heretical, incensed him. Rather than viewing the revivals as the commencement of the Last Days, Chauncy compared them to the tumult in his own church during the infamous Antinomian Controversy of the 1630s, another time of religious turmoil, when the colony banished prophetess Anne Hutchinson and other dissidents to Rhode Island. They were exiled from the Massachusetts Bay Colony because they believed that, as members of the elect, God dwelled within them and thus made their own judgments more binding than any man-made laws.[19] "*Few,*" Chauncy wrote, "*will venture to disown a* Likeness between the Disturbances then and now: *They are indeed surprisingly similar.*"[20]

If Chauncy was correct, in Edwards's way lay the same kind of social and political ruptures and communal scars that had marked the Massachusetts Bay Colony for a generation following Hutchinson's trial and banishment. But if Edwards's predictions were correct, everything else was moot. From his vantage point, all good, all harmony and purpose, would be answered by the dawning Millennium.

But Chauncy reminded his readers that, although biblical prophecy undeniably foretold that in good time God would make "this Earth a *Paradise,*" it was not for mankind to know how or precisely when this would occur. "Whoever pretend to such Knowledge," he observed, "are wise above what is written." Although "they think they may know much, they really know nothing as to this Matter." To reinforce his criticism, Chauncy cited a letter he had received from a "worthy Gentleman," presumably someone in the Connecticut Valley who took issue with Edwards's views. This correspondent claimed that Edwards had often said privately that "the *Millennium* began in NORTHHAMPTON 8 Years past" and so his congregation "must have the Praise of being first brought into" God's work.[21]

Edwards was incensed. This report from a single anonymous person—someone "concealed and kept behind the curtain"—painted him as presumptuous and arrogant. In a letter two years later to a colleague in Scotland, he still fumed. "It has been slanderously reported and printed concerning me," he wrote, that "I have often said that the Millennium was already begun, and that it began in Northampton."[22] While he had surmised that the revivals were likely part of God's plan in the history of redemption, he told William McCullough that he had never claimed explicitly that the "Little Awakening" in Northampton was initiating the Last Days.

Yet Edwards undeniably believed that the revivals promoted a more civil and pious society, and thus might be considered part of God's unfolding plan for humanity. But how could the results be made permanent? Beginning with his account of the positive behavioral changes that he had witnessed in the mid-1730s and his attempts further to institutionalize them, Edwards elaborated how the good society might cohere and flourish. He grounded his vision of an earthly "*Paradise*" in an ethic of profound Christian charity and equality that Chauncy and other Old Lights resisted, tied as they were to a model of social organization based on a static, hierarchical society that reinforced their own prominence.

If Edwards was correct, if in fact thousands of his converts had initiated an era of Christian charity, there was no social or political problem that could not be solved. But if he was wrong, as Chauncy believed, the revivals would weaken and perhaps shatter the security and structure of the clerical authority he and his cohort regarded as essential to social stability. To Chauncy, order depended on the wisdom of citizens as learned and accomplished as he, not on the presumption of Edwards or of deluded souls like Davenport and his illiterate followers.

Envisioning the Good Society

In a few years Whitefield's and other New Lights' revivals dwarfed the events of 1734 to 1735. Edwards's congregation among those reawakened, he did not want a repetition of what had occurred when a decade earlier Satan had destroyed all his labors. Thus, in 1742, he tried to institutionalize the revivals' positive results by drafting a new church covenant for his congregation. In it, he outlined how a people touched by the Spirit should behave toward each other. The document defined the good society to which regenerate mankind should aspire.

A few years earlier, Edwards had broached this subject in *Charity and Its Fruits*, taking as his primary text 1 Corinthians 13:1–8: "By their fruits ye shall know them." Commencing with a sermon on "Love the Sum of All Virtue" and concluding with "Heaven Is a World of Love," the series outlined the goal of the new covenant: to unite people in an ethic of Christian charity that reflects the glory of heaven. "Love is in God as light is in the sun," he observed, and flows out in innumerable streams toward all His creation. When a true convert shares his new sense of love with everyone around him, he more closely approaches the heaven for which he yearns.

Because love "always meets with answerable returns of love," it is axiomatic that one's charity will be reciprocated. Once God's love is at work in the world, matters inevitably move in the direction of a more Christian society. Every other problem, whether inordinate selfishness, "frolicking," excessive political partisanship, or lusting after ever-more-scarce pastureland, is of necessity resolved. When all rejoice in each other's happiness, there is no room for envy. God's love (and its human reflection) does not promise marginally improved social harmony. It changes things absolutely.[23]

Such a blessed state, Edwards wrote, inclines "the heart to flow out in love to God's people." Those with such an enlarged spirit are not concerned with themselves but live for the good of the church of God in general. Consider, too, he urged, how a professing Christian is united to Christ as well as to his fellow Christians, so that they all make one body, "Christ the head and Christians the members." And because the immediate seat of grace is the faculty of will that determines a person's actions, genuine conversion initiates moral reformation. All true grace would tend to holy action until selfless love filled the world. If heaven "be such a blessed world," he urged, "then let this be our chosen country, and the inheritance we seek."[24]

The implication was clear: if people practiced disinterested charity, the result would mirror heaven, "a garden of love, the Paradise of God, where everything has a cast of holy love, and everything conspires to promote and stir up love, and nothing to interrupt its exercises." Around him, however, Edwards still saw people of "pride and malice and contention and perpetual jarring." Fortunately, he had identified the solution—revival—for people to eliminate such behavior at a stroke. By participating in the social harmony engendered in a new awakening, Edwards counseled, one is "in the way to heaven" because, "as heaven is a world of love, so the way to heaven is the way of love."[25] No elaborate social reorganization other than bountiful charity is necessary.

Edwards centered his church's new covenant on this foundational premise. All in his congregation over fourteen years of age—hundreds of parishioners—swore allegiance to a new covenant. "Adoring the glorious Majesty, Power and Grace of God," Edwards wrote, "manifested in the present wonderful outpouring of his Spirit," and lamenting their "past backslidings and ungrateful departings from God," the congregation promised reformation. In all their "conversations, concerns and dealings" with their neighbors, they swore to a strict regard for honesty, justice, and uprightness. Members of the congregation would not defraud their neighbors. Nor would they "feed a spirit of bitterness, ill will, or secret grudge" against any neighbor or "insist on his real faults needlessly." People would stop their headlong tumble into selfishness and realize their true end, to love each other unreservedly.[26]

The new covenant targeted the divisive partisan politics tearing apart the province as good land became scarcer, for corn and cattle were at the root of much of the pervasive bickering in Northampton and elsewhere in the Connecticut Valley. As Northampton's population grew, access to fertile agricultural and grazing land became the main pathway to wealth. Because they grew corn to fatten cattle for the burgeoning Boston market, the community's largest taxpayers demanded (and usually received) deference commensurate with their prominence in local and provincial politics, while others struggled to subsist. By the 1740s, all of the common lands had been allotted. The only way a young person could improve his lot was through inheritance or purchase, both of which required his waiting for a longer time than usual to strike out on his own.[27]

In addition to being careful to avoid doing "any thing to our neighbour from a spirit of revenge," the congregation also promised not to disgrace their religion through pursuit of any "private interest," nor by forwarding their "own honour" or aligning themselves against "those of a contrary party." They foreswore making worldly gain their chief object. Nor would they fall into "unchristian bitterness, vehemence, or heat of spirit," even if they thought they were the injured party. Edwards and his congregants also understood that the realization of such a heaven on earth required their sincerest efforts. Although keeping these solemn vows might "be very contrary to our corrupt inclinations, and carnal interests," in this moving ceremony, with all other parishioners and God as witnesses, they promised to renounce all self-interest, the visible sign of original sin.[28]

Edwards's vision offered a policy prescription of sorts. He and his congregation recognized the larger town's shortcomings and chose to address them head-on. For despite the revivals of the mid-1730s and the glimpses of Zion's glory they offered, Northampton had remained a rat pit of envy and bitterness. Shortly after taking office, Edwards remarked long-standing contention between two parties in town who always "prepared to oppose one another in public affairs." Years later, in a letter to a correspondent in Scotland, he elaborated. During Stoddard's pastorate, Edwards wrote, there had been "some mighty contests and controversies" that even the patriarch could not control. Once, after a member of one group "unmercifully" attacked the leader of the opposing party, "the heat of the spirit was raised to such a height," that it "came to hard blows."[29]

This division of the people into two parties, he explained, was "somewhat like the Court and Country party in England."[30] By 1700 the richest 10 percent of men in Northampton controlled a quarter of the land, with the poorest 10 percent holding only 2 percent. With little common lands left, those at the lower end of the economic scale had little hope of bettering themselves. Edwards accurately described the "Court" party as composed of men "of chief authority and wealth, that have been great proprietors of their lands," and the other party, those "who have been jealous of them, apt to envy them, and afraid of their having too much power and influence in town and church."[31] His solution was not to urge compromise between the two groups but rather to insist that *all* must exercise Christian charity to *everyone*.

With the erosion of the communal, agrarian ethos on which Northampton was founded, townspeople, replicating trends appearing throughout the province of Massachusetts Bay, grew more concerned with their economic situation than with the state of their souls. With loans now available from colonial banks that accepted land as collateral, speculative men invested in livestock and yet more land, while smaller landowners looked on enviously. Credit became a commodity like any other: the more of it that one commanded, the more probable one's economic success. To preserve the very different spiritual good that the revivals had nurtured, Edwards urged his people to swear to the new church covenant, based as it was on an ethic of love and forbearance.

Truly Gracious Affections

Within a year, the general awakenings faltered, in large part because Chauncy's well-organized cohort so effectively attacked their validity. Intellectual jousting, however, continued for two more years, with the

Old Lights' criticism answered by Edwards and other New Light ministers who sent reports of local revivals to a new religious periodical, the *Christian History*. Edwards studied the accounts presented therein and in 1746 fired another volley. He published a series of sermons (preached in 1742 and 1743), under the title *A Treatise Concerning Religious Affections*, which eventually proved the most influential of all his writings.

Strategically, Edwards did not directly target either Chauncy or the Old Lights. Instead, he addressed a more fundamental and immediate concern, how the putative convert could know whether he or she was truly regenerated. Edwards knew that the risk of false affections or emotions, encouraged by Satan, remained real and pressing. More importantly, he insisted that truly gracious affections could not fail to produce transformational results. All the other problems—the censuring, the cries and swoons, the visions, the ranting of lay exhorters, the church schisms—stemmed from peoples' inability to discern true spiritual transformation. Too many congregants had grown complacent, resting comfortably in the belief that they were among the saints, and deceived themselves into thinking that they were growing in grace. As a consequence, the broader regenerative work that earlier had accompanied the revivals ceased, replaced by the envy and bitterness that had only briefly receded at the height of the fervor. Edwards knew that it was difficult to judge impartially of these matters in the midst of the dust and smoke of current controversies, but he thought it crucial to establish once and for all the criteria for church membership.

His prescription to heal Northampton's tensions lay in the encouragement and promulgation of truly gracious affections. These were not mere emotions or passions but the very core of peoples' motivation and thus of their very being. Affections were nothing less than "the more rigorous and sensible exercises of the inclination and will of the soul."[32]

Here, as elsewhere, Edwards took pains to distinguish between the mere *understanding*, by which man "discerns and judges of things," and the *will*. The will is the faculty, he explained, by which the soul does not just receive things but that which is "inclined" to what it views or considers, "either is inclined to 'em, or is disinclined, and averse from 'em." A person does not consider things—say, the opportunity to purchase more land—"as an indifferent unaffected spectator, but either as liking or disliking, [being] pleased or displeased, approving or rejecting" this choice. Some people term this faculty the "*inclination*," he emphasized, "and the mind, with regard to the exercises of this faculty is often called the *heart*." The will and the affections thus are not distinct faculties but actually *one and the same*. These are "the springs that set men agoing," and the chief of these is comprehended in *love*, the "fountain of all other affections."[33]

"As on the one hand," Edwards counseled, "there must be light in the understanding, as well as an affected fervent heart, where there is heat without light, there can be nothing divine or heavenly in that heart." But conversely, "where there is a kind of light without heat, a head stored with notions and speculations, with a cold and unaffected heart, there can be nothing divine in that light, that knowledge is no true spiritual knowledge of divine things."[34] When people have true religion, they are *moved to act* in certain ascertainable ways. This is the crux, for when so moved, the truly religious person cannot help but engender and return love for love, good work for good work. If true revival continued, the problems afflicting both individual and society would, at a stroke, be resolved.

In his first sign of truly religious affections, Edwards returned to what he had treated so convincingly in "A Divine and Supernatural Light." Saints, he explained, have "a new inward perception or sensation" on their minds "entirely different in its nature and kind, from anything that ever their minds were the subjects of before they were sanctified." This new spiritual sense is a new *principle* in the saint, a natural habit or foundation for action so that it becomes part of one's nature, part of who one is, ever after. This "new, simple idea," as "some metaphysicians" (that is, John Locke and his followers) call it, transforms one's sense of heart, one's basic character. With it, the sinner becomes a saint.[35]

Much follows the saint's apprehension of this new, simple idea. For one thing, the individual sees the "transcendentally excellent and amiable nature of divine things as they are," not through any relation they may have to one's self-interest. The regenerated person acquires a certain divine spiritual taste. As a result, one perceives something so different from what natural people experience "as the sweet taste of honey is diverse from the ideas men get of honey by looking on it or feeling of it."[36]

A sense of beautiful symmetry and proportion also accompanies conversion, demonstrated when the saint displays love toward others and manifests his piety in various ways toward *all* creation in a beautiful, consistent way. While hypocrites are "like the waters in a time of a shower of rain," which then "run like a brook, and flow abundantly" but later become dry, the true saint "is like a stream from a living spring" that flows faster after rain or less in drought but that *constantly* flows.[37]

The results are not only consistent but also forever increasing. The more a true saint loves God, Edwards explained, the more one desires to love him more. Conversely, Edwards cautioned that complacency was the surest sign of one's sinfulness, for the saint's behavior always tends toward goodness, "as bodies [that] are attracted to the globe of the earth, tend to it more strongly, the nearer they come to the attracting body, and are not at rest out of the center."[38]

Edwards had read his Newton: the larger the mass, the greater the number of the regenerate, the stronger their attraction. Edwards connected this gravitational metaphor to a final sign: gracious and holy affections have "their exercise and fruit in Christian practice," so that the saint becomes a center of goodness who draws others to his or her cause (as had occurred time after time in the revivals). Christian *practice*, Edwards maintained, is "the chief of all the evidences of a saving sincerity in religion."[39]

Exile to Stockbridge

Unfortunately, despite Edwards's effort to bring heaven to earth, he experienced little of this saintly harmony. He and his congregation first bickered about salary; as his family grew, Northampton was slow to increase his allotment. Then, a few years later, he rethought the qualifications for admission to church membership and the sacrament of communion. During the awakenings, he had accepted as adequate mere assent to the cardinal points of Christian doctrine, a practice his grandfather Stoddard had instituted decades before and that had become widespread in New England. But with the awakening in a shambles, Edwards wondered if he should insist on more convincing evidence before approving church members. He decided to reinstitute the requirement for a personal profession of faith, including a description of an experience of saving grace, a test that once had been common in the Massachusetts Bay Colony but that Stoddard and many others subsequently had rejected as unscriptural.

At a practical level, Edwards was just trying to make sure that those approved for the communion table did in fact more than just assent to certain Christian principles: they had to make visible their changed hearts through their constant commitment to Christian charity. For a while after Edwards announced the change, no one came forward for consideration. When one did, in 1748, he abruptly changed his mind, saying that, according to long-established rules in the church, such a profession was unnecessary. There followed "great uneasiness" in the congregation, and when Edwards asked permission to preach on the matter to explain his reasoning, he met a firestorm of criticism. Another candidate said that she was willing to abide by the new procedure; but she, too, demurred, "afraid, by what she had heard, that there would be a tumult if she came into the church that way."[40] By challenging Stoddard's loose admission standards, Edwards had incurred the wrath of many townspeople.

He tried to explain his position in his *Humble Inquiry into the Word of God Concerning the Qualifications Requisite to a Complete Standing and Full Communion in the Visible Christian Church*, but hardly anyone in Northampton paid any attention.[41] That same year, disaffected church members asked a council of neighboring churches to decide whether Edwards should be dismissed for his departure from his church's long-held principles. Early in the summer of 1750, by a vote of ten to nine, the council recommended separation. As Samuel Hopkins, one of Edwards's protégés and first biographer, wrote, it was a "sorrowful, strange, surprising affair."[42]

Edwards now faced the prospect of finding another position, even as he realized that to many churches he was no longer desirable or even acceptable. He admitted as much in a letter to the Reverend Thomas Foxcroft even before the council had rendered its decision. "I have many enemies abroad in the country, who hate me for my stingy principles, enthusiasm, rigid proceedings, and that now are expecting full triumph over me," he confided. To his Scots correspondent John Erskine, he was equally honest. "I am now as it were thrown upon the wide ocean of the world and know not what will become of me and my numerous and chargeable family." Hopkins agreed: "beggary, as well as disgrace, stared him [Edwards] full in the face."[43] His prospects slim, later that year Edwards accepted an offer from the Commissioners for Indian Affairs in Boston to become missionary to the Native Americans in the frontier settlement of Stockbridge, Massachusetts, fifty miles west of Northampton in Berkshire County.

God's End in Creation

Edwards spent the next seven years in exile in Stockbridge, preaching to a few-score of white settlers in English and to Mahican Indians through a translator. Remarkably, these years in the wilderness marked the zenith of his intellectual achievement, for there he penned four treatises that put him in conversation with Europe's most advanced philosophers and theologians. Two of these, his *Careful and Strict Inquiry into the Modern Prevailing Notions of . . . Freedom of the Will* and *The Great Christian Doctrine of Original Sin Defended*, are still considered virtually irrefutable discussions of their subjects. The other two are profoundly ethical writings that add significantly to our understanding of Edwards's view of a just and moral society and indicate that, despite his disappointment, he did not abandon his wish to make earth reflect heaven. The two pieces were published together shortly after his death as *Two Dissertations: Concerning the End for Which God Created the World* [and] *The Nature of True Virtue* (1765). They reveal an Edwards who now had the time to tackle the thorniest metaphysical questions in ways that extended his thoughts on the relationship of divine regeneration to social reform.

God's actions, Edwards had opined in his *Freedom of the Will*, "are in the highest, most absolutely perfect manner virtuous and praiseworthy"; they are so, he reasoned, "because they are most perfectly necessary."[44] But "necessary" for what? Why did God dispose of things as he did? In *The End*, Edwards explained that the whole universe, including all creatures "animate and inanimate," in all its "actings, proceeding, revolutions, and entire series of events," proceeds "from a regard and with a view to God, as the supreme and last end of all."[45]

Edwards saved for this work's companion treatise an answer to what such an understanding of God's creation demands of his creatures, but one important implication was that, because virtue and holiness are God's very substance, God constantly distributes more of the same throughout the universe, including to his human creations. When people act in agreement with this holiness, they fulfill their highest purpose. But in so doing, Edwards noted, they do not *add* to God's luster but only *exemplify* it.

Giving ourselves to God through selfless worship and charitable behavior is integral to his intention, for when one yearns to be with God, one acknowledges not one's own but God's will. Not to yearn to be part of this "remanation" blatantly marks a sinful disposition, a sense of heart at cross-purposes with God's intentions. "God's respect to the creature's good, and his respect to himself" are not different matters, Edwards explained. Rather, both are "united in one," and the happiness of the creature aimed at is "happiness in union with [God] himself."[46]

Edwards left his most profound and challenging insight for the final pages of this treatise. Because creation is ongoing and eternal, he wrote, the time will never come when one can say that his or her union with God is complete. The saint consequently will never know God as perfectly as one desires. Just as God aims at satisfying justice in the damnation of sinners, so he glorifies his saints in heaven with "eternal felicity," bestowing upon them "a good infinitely valuable." Yet "there never will come the moment, when it can be said, that now this infinitely valuable good has been actually bestowed."[47] Just as eternity is central to the end for which God created the world, so the saint's life consists of constant movement toward an ever-distant center.

Why did it matter that Jonathan Edwards sought to explain the saint's eternal striving for God's unreachable goodness? What difference did it make to the inhabitants of Stockbridge or Northampton, or anywhere else besides? Practically speaking, it grounded in metaphysical terms the notion of a Christian's constant growth in grace. Complacency, self-satisfaction, and spiritual pride represented the other side of this coin. The Christian race is never-ending, and striving to enter the strait gate requires a constant exercise of one's will: there is no sitting still. Edwards sought to inculcate an ethic of continual movement toward a divine goal, whose result would be a world of social harmony.

Another question naturally arises: What constitutes true goodness, a virtuous and moral life? For Edwards, the answer was closely linked to his discussion, in the *Freedom of the Will*, of one's *disposition*—that is, of how one *sees* the world—as a saint inclined to gracious behavior, or a sinner motivated by self-interest? Edwards addressed the implications of this struggle in *The Nature of True Virtue*. He proposed that true virtue essentially consists of "benevolence to Being in general" that is "immediately exercised in a general good will."[48]

God created man to reflect God's presence in everyday life, and the best evidence of such reciprocated love, Edwards declared, arises from the temper of mind that consists in "a supreme propensity of [one's] heart to God," what we might term a supernal longing. It is our loving consent to "*God's end* in our creation and in the creation of all things" and our desire to replicate in all aspects of our lives "the *manner* in which *God* himself exercises love to the creature."[49] This is what Edwards meant, in his companion dissertation, when he wrote that God had created the world so that humankind might reflect His glory.

Even in Stockbridge, however, Edwards could not escape the political machinations that had hampered and then ended his tenure in Northampton. Charged with the oversight of a boarding school for Native Americans, he found himself constantly arguing with his supervisors in Boston as well as with the ambitious Williams family—the same family that led the opposition to him in Northampton—who wanted to take over the school. Edwards eventually gained the commissioners' confidence, winning this round against the Williamses. Then, in 1757, he received a surprising invitation.

Five years earlier a young Presbyterian (and prorevival) minister, Aaron Burr, father of the future vice president, had traveled from his home in New Jersey to seek the hand of one of Edwards's daughters. By the time they were married, Burr had been named president of the College of New Jersey, founded as a seminary to train New Light clergy, and an institution that Edwards knew and supported. To Burr's delight early in 1757—he had been there for a decade—a sizable religious revival broke out. But his indefatigable work for the school took a toll on his health, and that same year he died of malaria, leaving a widow ten years younger than he. The college offered his position to his father-in-law. Who better to run the school than the colonies' most renowned revivalist?

Although urged on by his friend and fellow minister William Tennent, Edwards did not immediately accept the offer. He worried about uprooting his family when they were now comfortable in Stockbridge. He also wondered if he was suited for the post. In a lengthy self-analysis, he laid before the trustees a laundry list of reasons why he was not qualified for the proffered position.[50] Despite his honest assessment of his unfitness, the college's trustees convinced him and quickly installed Edwards as its third president.

Their joy was short-lived. When an outbreak of smallpox occurred, Edwards assented to inoculation. But the treatment was in its infancy and the dosage not easily controlled. His was excessive, and a few days after its administration, he contracted the disease and lingered painfully for a month. Three months after moving to Princeton he was gone.

Immediate Legacy

In his short life Jonathan Edwards already had indelibly marked American religious and cultural history. He urged men and women to understand that genuine Christian charity would lead them closer and closer to their highest end, to reflect the glory of God on earth as they move eternally toward union with him. After Edwards's death, under pressure from more liberal clergy who disagreed with him on several theological matters, his two chief disciples, Joseph Bellamy and Samuel Hopkins, subtly reinterpreted and in some cases altered his writings. If, for Edwards, the height of one's piety consisted in seeking to reflect the transcendent deity, Bellamy and Hopkins, confronted with attacks from more liberal clergy, centered Christian duty more in this world and on its human inhabitants.

These two theologians' works contributed to the gradual secularization of American religious thought that resulted in part from the increasing influence in the colonies of Enlightenment philosophy.[51] Latitudinarian theologians and philosophers in England and on the Continent argued that one could understand nature and mankind best through the use of one's natural faculties, particularly reason. These thinkers embraced what physics, chemistry, and biology taught and showed how such discoveries supported the notion of divine order: one deduced the existence and substance of God by studying his creation. In the words of Locke, one of the age's chief philosophers, through close observation of the natural world, one understood the *reasonableness* of Christianity. This also allowed one to discern the components of a moral life and, when working with other enlightened citizens, consequently to build a society whose central premise was the happiness of the greatest number.

Challenged by the ideas of those who believed that one should use his intelligence to forward the general happiness of humanity rather than to ponder a finally unknowable deity, Bellamy and Hopkins struggled to square scripture with this "natural religion." The dialogue between them and American liberal clergy, influenced as well by such English latitudinarian theologians as Samuel Clarke and Archbishop John Tillotson, reveals the first, tentative emergence of a branch of Christianity that by the early nineteenth century eventuated in very different religious emphases, a faith in which social harmony could be achieved without divine guidance but instead realized through human effort.

After the 1750s, with the torrents of revival shrunk to rivulets, some clergy rejected Edwards's theology for its sheer abstruseness, arguing, as Harriet Beecher Stowe later wrote, that this brilliant thinker had constructed a beautiful ladder to the heavens, climbed it, and then pulled it up after him.[52] By midcentury Edwards's Calvinist notions of original sin and freedom of the will seemed more and more irrational and thus implausible, as concern for each individual's inherent natural gifts became more relevant than the irrevocable decrees of a distant, mystical deity.

Edwards's stands as the high-water mark of an intellectually rigorous, God-centered solution to the problem of social harmony, but a more secularly accommodating set of ideas and practices was necessary if people were to realize, by eighteenth-century standards, an enlightened society. The times demanded a *reasoned* response to the political, economic, and social upheaval that culminated in the Revolutionary War and the founding of the United States. How did Edwards's notion of true virtue help the farmer who joined the Continental army to fight against King George and then, after the Revolutionary War, learned that the new nation could not afford his pension? How did the Christian deity fit into the new Constitution's prohibition of the government's making any law regarding the establishment of religion, or how was God relevant to the political bitterness that marked the presidential election of 1800? Such questions and many others swirling around them, Edwards's successors valiantly attempted to salvage his legacy, even as they subtly modified his central ideas.

Joseph Bellamy (1719–1790) had known him the longest, having been his first theological pupil when, shortly after graduation from Yale in 1736, he had traveled to Northampton and asked for tutorial.[53] There he studied scripture, read theology, wrote sermons, and accompanied his tutor on pastoral visits. Licensed to preach in 1737, three years later Bellamy began a ministry in what became the western Connecticut town of Bethlehem. He remained there for fifty years and in his rustic study trained more young men in divinity than any other New England clergyman of his generation.

Bellamy had arrived in Northampton just after the "Little Awakening" and had thus experienced firsthand the effects of the surprising conversions. In the winter of 1738–1739 his own parish experienced a comparable revival. With Whitefield's arrival in New England in 1740, Bellamy's church again grew exponentially: "Every man, woman, and child, about 6 years old and upwards," Bellamy wrote, was "under religious concern." All "quarrels were ended, and frolicks flung up." As in Edwards's Northampton, prayer meetings proliferated and "matters of religion were all the talk."[54]

Bellamy was well suited to oversee such work. His biographers agree that he outshone Edwards as a preacher and even rivaled the great Whitefield. He was imposing—six feet tall, slender, with a booming voice and a tendency to colorful language, he was known for his acerbic wit and penchant for using homespun anecdotes in his sermons. Volatile and pugnacious, he was a fierce debater in religious controversies. Ezra Stiles, an Old Light opponent, remembered him as "boisterous & vociferous in Preaching, of a dogmatical & overbearing Disposition, severe, rigid & uncharitable."[55]

Initially not as discriminating about the revivals as Edwards, by the mid-1740s, he met a barrage of criticism for New Light excesses. Such attacks came most frequently from an emergent group of liberal Christians led by Boston clergymen Charles Chauncy. He and other recent

Harvard graduates had read their Clarke and Tillotson and championed a broader view of church membership based solely on rational assent to scripture's moral truths.[56] They championed an enlarged and optimistic view of mankind's abilities, including a belief that the doctrine of original sin as generally taught—that it was present in all men and women from birth—was spurious, and that through one's natural efforts—one's free will—one could ensure salvation.

Strict Calvinists termed such views "Arminianism," after the seventeenth-century Dutch theologian Jacobus Arminius, who had widely promulgated them. Bellamy took to his study to ponder the "delusions" that were beginning to divide the Christian world. Over his lengthy ministry, he reinforced, reinterpreted, and reoriented evangelical Christianity, subtly shifting his mentor's understanding of man's highest end from a desire for mystical closure with God to the living of a strictly moral life.

Bellamy first mined the vein that Edwards had in his *Religious Affections*—how to distinguish true religion from false. In 1750 he published *True Religion Delineated*, the substance of which he had earlier preached to his flock. For him true religion did not consist in the mystical sense of benevolence that Edwards had described. Bellamy asserted, rather, that it consisted in conformity to the *law* of God as revealed in the Gospels.[57] That law is perfectly fulfilled, Bellamy believed, in the exercise of love on this earth. But one loved God not for his unapproachable beauty but for his role as the supreme lawgiver, the moral governor of the world.

While Edwards spoke of utter joy at God's supernal beauty as the mark of true regeneration, Bellamy thought this test too subjective. He emphasized instead a recognition of "the intrinsic moral fitness of the law."[58] With a nod to the Enlightenment's respect for natural law, he argued that the Bible commanded a love of God because God's moral law was synonymous with what man discerned in the natural world. The law of Mount Sinai, he explained, was nothing more than a new and plainer edition of the laws of nature. Nature thus demonstrated and reinforced scriptural law as objectively and universally valid, and therefore people could, and should, live by it. To do so was the clearest sign that their affections were genuine.

This emphasis on personal liberty is also visible in Bellamy's discussion of self-interest. With Edwards, he believed that any affections that were "for *self-ends*" were spurious. But while Edwards posited the necessary change from selfishness to selflessness as dependent on God's free grace, Bellamy believed that one should habitually *practice* benevolence because Mosaic law demanded it, an implicit capitulation to the notion that people themselves had the power to become holy, something close to Arminianism. The *law* demanded that we ought to be "*perfectly benevolent*" toward neighbors, "to rejoice in their prosperity, and be grieved for their adversity," all from "a cordial love and genuine good-will." Self-love only led people to be jealous of their neighbors' prosperity and to experience "*hard-heartedness* in the time of [their] adversity," evident when neighbors envied the economically successful but smugly ignored them if they experienced financial distress. Now, Bellamy observed, too many people "set up for [them]selves, to make [their] own interest [their] last end." Everyone goes "his way, one to his farm, another to his merchandize, all serving divers lusts and pleasures."[59]

Bellamy's subtle shifts of emphasis are significant. Rather than consent to the way the universe *is*, in its totality, he emphasized the convert's consent to the good of *human beings* as the chief evidence of saintliness, a verification of the law's natural fitness. Gone was Edwards's ideal of a union of the human will with a transcendent deity. One respected the glory of God by respect for the moral law, evincing goodness to one's friends and neighbors.

Until his last decade, when he suffered a stroke, Bellamy remained a formidable controversialist, battling against the growing power of the liberal clergy as well as the "Old Calvinists" who defended a more diluted, if more reasonable, view of Calvinism's chief principles—they questioned, for example, whether a benevolent God could be the author of sin. Acknowledging Bellamy's prominence, Yale president Ezra Stiles, an important member of this more moderate group, derisively called him the "Pope of Litchfield County" and regretted the number of recent Yale graduates who had found their way to his study.[60] But Bellamy's legalism, his sense of disinterested love visible only in social harmony, and his calculation of virtue in terms of the happiness of the greatest number, set him off from his mentor. His own tutees' widespread adoption of his views testified to their applicability in this new age in which individual liberty and "rational" religion were ascendant.

Bellamy refashioned Calvinism for the Revolutionary era. He realized that Arminianism liberated its adherents to cultivate guilt-free self-interest in a burgeoning market economy. His focus on the moral law and its social applicability provided a middle way, as he urged his followers to love their neighbor as the best way to love God. Beneath all his contributions, though, continued to bubble and seethe the question of the true extent of human liberty in an era in which many were celebrating the individual's centrality in new ways.

From the New Divinity to Liberal Christianity

Samuel Hopkins, a native of Waterbury, Connecticut, was two and a half years younger than Bellamy and, like him, had attended Yale College.[61] He, too, had heard Whitefield preach at Yale and watched as he subsequently ignited the whole region. Then, at Hopkins's commencement in 1742, Edwards delivered *The Distinguishing Marks of the Work of the Spirit.* He "had before read Edwards's sermons on Justification, &c., and his Narrative of the Remarkable Conversions," Hopkins remembered, but he was more impressed by this address as by any of Edwards's other works. Like Bellamy, he decided to study with him in Northampton.

In 1743 the newly established town of Housatonic (later, Great Barrington), Massachusetts, a few miles from where Bellamy was settled in northwestern Connecticut, called Hopkins as its minister. He held this position for the next twenty-five years. His forte was polemical theology. Like Edwards, he assiduously read the latest European philosophical and theological works. One neighbor remembered that when, as a child, he had met Hopkins, the minister would ask the boy's name, and that of his father, but "never seemed to notice my answers so as to recollect them, but appeared to be *lost in divinity*." Hopkins was remembered as so "thoroughly honest" that a "*sobriquet*" often applied to him later in his life, even by his enemies, was "Old Sincerity."[62]

Hopkins occasionally preached to the Native Americans at nearby Stockbridge, and on the death of their minister, John Sergeant, was asked to replace him. Hopkins demurred but recommended a close friend and mentor in need of a job, Jonathan Edwards. Hopkins thus had the good fortune to live near his two best friends, Bellamy and Edwards, until the latter's call to Princeton in 1758. He himself remained in Berkshire County until 1769, when after difficulties with his congregation over salary and other local matters ended in his dismissal, he accepted a position in the seaport town of Newport, Rhode Island, one of New England's commercial centers. Hopkins remained there for the rest of his career, and having caught the contagion of liberty, distinguished himself as one of the region's strongest antislavery voices in a community that had long profited from the slave trade.

Like Bellamy, Hopkins adapted his mentor's ideas for the post-Revolutionary period. His interventions were threefold. He claimed that God's power is so absolute that he does not just permit sin but does so all the better to show his glory in salvation, that there was "God's wisdom in the permission of sin." Second, he argued that, if one is not genuinely converted, such exercises as prayer, attendance on sermons, and Bible study are insignificant; if one refuses to give one's heart to God, all else that one does is wicked. More controversially yet, Hopkins also declared that disinterested benevolence requires such self-sacrifice that one should be willing to be damned for the glory of God.

Like Bellamy, Hopkins sought to make his Calvinist scheme more reasonable, and palatable, to an audience increasingly unwilling to tolerate a theology that seemed to flout the laws of nature and common sense and did not have mankind's interests at its center. The age embraced humanitarianism, a belief that men and women themselves could make the world better. Many Christians were less interested in speculating on the nature of divinity than on their rights and liberties as free individuals. Government's purpose was not to initiate a world of Christian charity but rather to ensure a general content and prosperity. So long as one did not impede others from achieving comparable independence and success, one was in line with Gospel truth.

Edwards and his New Divinity followers strove mightily to resist this rising tide and did so with the most potent tool they knew—revivalism. But their renovated Calvinism alone could not beat back what by 1800 had become inexorable. Edwards had urged an ecstatic relation of the individual to God; his successors, profitable relations among people. Led by such liberals as Chauncy, Ebenezer Gay, and other clergy who prided themselves as being au courant the latest Enlightenment thought and principles, the new generation urged an understanding, rationally arrived at, of the dignity and value of each individual. This emergent liberal group substituted one's rational understanding of Christ's moral character for the arbitrary will of God. For each person's sinful nature, they substituted a universal common sense—advocated by such Scots philosophers as Thomas Reid, Adam Ferguson, and Dugald Stewart—that might occasion sin but also could turn away from it at will. Thus, in place of free, irresistible grace, they substituted one's universal moral ability to become a better Christian.

Chauncy and his followers thought that the New Divinity men subordinated religion's social utility to dry metaphysical speculation. Their growing cadre was, above all else, now avowedly Arminian. They openly asserted that people had the capacity to be either good or evil, and through their own efforts and God's assistance, they could overcome their disposition to sin. They also believed that human reason supported the essentials of religion—the existence of God and the requirements of morality. Finally, as the century wore on, some in this group even questioned whether scriptural, and rational, evidence supported a Trinitarian God—Father, Son, and Holy Spirit.

The liberal faction developed these ideas largely through their engagement with proponents of New Divinity over such issues as the meaning and purpose of sin, the nature of benevolence, God's intention in creating the world, and man's role in the attainment of divine grace. Once again, Chauncy was at the forefront of the battles, just as forty years earlier he had sparred with Edwards. For years he had harbored more liberal religious views, but he kept them hidden until the 1780s. But now the time was right. In *The Benevolence of the Deity*, written in the 1750s but not published until 1784, he argued that God's goodness is central to his greatness, which expresses itself most visibly in his benevolence to humankind, benevolence defined as "a principle disposing and prompting to the communication of happiness." Unlike Edwards, who insisted on the great distance between the individual and God, Chauncy shrunk it, claiming that God's benevolence is simply the same as what people exercise toward each other, though greater in degree. "Every Being, in heaven and earth, to whom this attribute may be applied," he wrote, "partakes of the *same quality*, though not in the same *manner*, nor in the same *degree* and *proportion*" as what God exercises.[63] This is another way of saying that God's moral government exists for the progressive happiness of humanity.

Another manuscript that Chauncy prepared in the 1750s but held for more than thirty years was *The Mystery Hid from the Ages and Generations, Made Manifest by the Gospel-Revelation; or, The Salvation of All Men the Grand Thing Aimed at in the Scheme of God*, which he published anonymously in London in 1784, no doubt aware that its radicalism would be condemned by many of his American counterparts. In this treatise, he positioned himself between the New Divinity men and a newly emergent group of Universalists centered around John Murray, who spread the notion that a benevolent God promised universal salvation. Murray spoke for those Christians who could not imagine a deity who would arbitrarily save or punish men and women, as Calvinists believed.

In his own work Chauncy argued that, because God formed human beings for their happiness, even if they fall into sin, they might pull themselves from it with the proper instigation. Damnation is real, he believed, but it consists of an intermediate state in which one continues to be drawn toward God. When they are free of their moral depravity and acquire a virtuous temper of mind, they will be saved. God designed damnation not for vengeance but for further reformation, for he loves all men and women and wishes their redemption.

The political as well as the philosophical ideas that marked the American Enlightenment help account for this theological shift from a God-centered universe to one that a benevolent deity created for human happiness. Now, reason and not revelation pointed to the great moral truths. Enlightenment thinkers posited a universe filled with hope for the individual's tendency to self-improvement, not despair over one's sinfulness. In Thomas Jefferson's words, what most mattered were life, liberty, and the pursuit of happiness. Government, as best defined in Madison, Jay, and Hamilton's *Federalist Papers*, existed to secure these goods for the greatest number, to guarantee that people are free to fulfill themselves in this world and not worry about the possibility of another.

Even more threatening was a new challenge, beginning in the 1770s, from a group of yet more radical thinkers collectively called deists. They threatened the very roots of Christian belief by acknowledging that there was an impersonal deity but denying that it ruled the universe in the personal way so many Christians believed. They were steeped in the philosophy of John Toland, Matthew Tindal, and Joseph Priestley among the English; and Montesquieu, Voltaire, and Jean-Jacques Rousseau on the Continent. Among its American exponents were not only Revolutionary War hero Ethan Allen and political pamphleteer Thomas Paine but also such Founding Fathers as Benjamin Franklin, Thomas Jefferson, and even George Washington, who had little use for organized Christianity but still recognized religion as the glue that, "of all the dispositions and habits which lead to political prosperity," was indispensable.[64] Old Calvinists like Stiles and

Timothy Dwight as well as Bellamy, Hopkins, and other New Divinity men (as they were called) shuddered at the prospect that the French Revolution would unleash even more such prophets whose poisonous radicalism would spread cross the Atlantic.

But despite threats from such various directions, these latitudinarians and radicals failed to push Edwards and the New Divinity men off the nation's ecclesiastical map. They remained at the center of a series of revivals from the 1790s to the 1830s, and their thought permeated popular culture.[65] In *The Minister's Wooing* (1859) Harriet Beecher Stowe put into the mouth of a central character based on Hopkins a defense of his theory of disinterested benevolence. In another novel, *Oldtown Folks* (1869), which drew on her husband's childhood years in Natick, Massachusetts, she again indicated how profoundly Edwards's thought animated everyday New Englanders. His works, she wrote, were "discussed by every farmer, in intervals of plough and hoe, by every woman and girl, at loom, spinning wheel, or wash-tub." New England, she continued, was "one vast sea, surging from depths to heights with thought and discussion on the most insoluble of mysteries." Writing earlier in the *Atlantic Monthly*, she sought to explain why. In New England, she wrote, "every man, woman, and child was more or less a theologian."[66]

Edwards's vision of heaven as a world of love persisted beyond Stowe well into the twentieth century. The neo-Calvinist theologian Reinhold Niebuhr understood how his predecessor viewed the relation between the aggrandizement of self and the good of society. "Nothing that is worth doing can be achieved in our lifetime," he wrote, so therefore "we must be saved by hope." And "nothing which is true or beautiful or good makes complete sense in any immediate context of history," so "therefore we must be saved by faith." But "nothing we do," he added, "however virtuous, can be accomplished alone," so, therefore, "we are saved by love."[67]

Few others in the two centuries after Edwards better understood the implications of Edwards's claim that heaven is a world of love and that humanity's purpose was to strive to imitate it. But back in

1830 this was not yet to be, for the stage was set for the emergence of another thinker as capacious as Edwards who offered a very different paradigm of social harmony to a young republic struggling with a new set of social and political challenges. Boundless self-reliance soon enough eclipsed Christian charity as young America's most distinctive trait.

2
Ralph Waldo Emerson

THE INFINITUDE OF THE COMMON MAN

Lyman Beecher Comes to Boston

Another liberal clergyman and erstwhile friend of Charles Chauncy, the Reverend Jonathan Mayhew, died in 1766, a decade before the break from England that he had begun to urge.[1] Charles Chauncy lived twenty-one years longer, through the founding of the new nation. In those two decades, the world was transformed. Immigration from Europe increased, with settlers now pushing up to and sometimes over the Appalachians. Everywhere there was talk of democratic rights frustrated by British officials' arrogance and greed. The king's emissaries were viewed as corrupt, intent on using their colonial sinecures as the means to enlarge their own prestige and fortunes. Beginning in 1775, outright warfare pitted family against family, and friend against friend, as some colonists remained loyal to the English crown, while others took up Patrick Henry's cry, "Give me liberty, or give me death."

Eventually, patriots formed a democratic republic based in Enlightenment guarantees of civil liberties and respect for human dignity. The country's foundational documents enshrined freedom of religion, even as the new nation remained avowedly Christian. It was a world roiled and transforming, with upheaval and confusion evident everywhere one looked, including in New England pulpits.

With the end of the Revolutionary War, Calvinists were split into several factions. The rubrics of "Old" and "New" Lights, though still in use, were complicated by the new ranks of Hopkinsians or New Divinity men and a cohort of "Old Calvinists" who claimed loyalty to the principles of the first settlers, even as they preached them in diluted form. Beginning in the 1770s this last group spawned another that grew increasingly important, those "liberal" Christians whose harbingers had been Lemuel Briant and Ebenezer Gay, as well as Chauncy and Mayhew.

This group passed a critical point in 1805 when Harvard College appointed the liberal Christian Henry Ware Sr. to the Hollis Professorship of Divinity. A year later the Harvard Corporation further infuriated conservatives by naming Samuel Webber to the vacant presidency of the school. For the next half-century, liberal Christians, who in 1819 openly adopted the moniker "Unitarians," ruled eastern New England's intellectual and religious life.[2]

But the New Divinity men and Old Calvinists did not go quietly. Numerous revivals in the 1790s in the western parts of Massachusetts and Connecticut demonstrated their fervor.[3] Nor did they relinquish eastern Massachusetts without a fight. The Reverend Jedediah Morse, a Yale graduate who had studied theology with Edwards's son Jonathan Jr. and in 1789 was installed in the Charlestown, Massachusetts, pulpit, right next door to Harvard, fought Ware's appointment tooth and nail. Failing in that effort, in 1807 he led a successful campaign to establish a rival theological school, the Andover Theological Seminary, thirty miles north of Boston. The fledging institution quickly became a destination for clergy who opposed Harvard's liberalization of Christianity. Nine years later, another group of conservative clergymen set new battle lines with the founding of the Bangor Theological Seminary, in what later became the state of Maine.[4]

The controversy over the Hollis Chair at Harvard was only the most visible of many religious controversies in these years. In 1811, Yale's dwindling Old Calvinist faction, increasingly jealous of the success of New Divinity men in other parts of New England, brought their troops right to the Boston Common with the appointment of Edward Dorr Griffin, another Yale graduate and later president of Williams College, to the elegant Park Street Church, just below the gilt dome of Charles Bulfinch's recently completed Massachusetts State House. Griffin quickly went on the offensive, giving a series of lectures (subsequently published in 1813 as *Lectures Delivered in Park Street Church, Boston, on Sabbath Evenings*) in which he attacked the innovations of the New Divinity men as well as those of the Unitarians. "You can form no adequate idea," he wrote shortly after his arrival at Park Street, "of the strength of Satan's kingdom in this town and its vicinity."[5]

Then, in 1825, flush from successful revivals in the western parts of New England and central New York, Hopkinsians laid siege to Boston, seeking to bring revivals right to the Unitarians' backyard. Some disgruntled members of the Old South Church and Park Street Church, chafing under ministries that were unresponsive to the awakenings, formed the Hanover Street Church, in Boston's North End, and chose as their first pastor the well-known revivalist Lyman Beecher (Harriet Beecher Stowe's father), who had played a central role in the western Connecticut awakenings.[6] A successful series of sermons he had given two years earlier at Old South had inspired dispirited Bostonians who wanted such preaching regularly. When the Hanover Street Church was formed, the parishioners recalled Beecher's fiery preaching and gave him the call.

Another Yale graduate, Beecher was the protégé of Yale's new president, Timothy Dwight, Jonathan Edwards's grandson and an important systematic theologian in his own right: his posthumously published five-volume *Theology Explained and Defended*, which he expounded to students in Sunday lectures, buttressed Edwards's legacy in the new century.[7] Before the call to Hanover Street, Beecher had labored in the small town of Litchfield in rural Connecticut, rustling up revivals in the area. He enjoyed this work but understood the Boston pulpit as centrally important to the defense of what, in one of his most famous sermons, Beecher called "the faith once delivered to the saints." "It is that New England is to be regenerated," he explained, "and the enemy driven out of the temple they have usurped and polluted, the college to be rescued, and the public sentiment revolutionized and restored to evangelical tone."[8]

And who were the chief polluters? Unlike Griffin a decade earlier,

Beecher was not about to start a catfight with fellow Calvinists. The problem was the newly victorious Unitarian ministers, young and "feeble" men, he explained, "who did not have the confidence and control of the population nominally under them as their predecessors had" but admittedly exercised considerable influence in ecclesiastical affairs. Thinking about the challenge of bringing the Gospel to New England's political, commercial, and Unitarian center, Beecher exclaimed: "It was as fire in my bones," adding, "my mind was all the time heating—heating—heating."[9]

Beecher linked his efforts in Boston to the millennial dreams of his Puritan ancestors. "All the great designs which God has to answer by planting our fathers here in this nation," he wrote, depended on "the efforts of this generation to rescue their institutions from perversion, and restore them to native purity and glory"—that is, to preserve Edwards's legacy in newly developed form.[10] There in Boston, where the Puritans first settled, Beecher would begin this restoration, "an undivided and renovated effort for the extension of religious and moral influence throughout the land."[11] While the Unitarians were content to preach morality and ethics, Beecher called for a return to Gospel truths and the Calvinist doctrine they engendered. In another famous sermon, *The Bible as a Code of Laws* (1817), he bellowed, "the law of the Lord is perfect, adapted to the exigencies of a lost world."[12]

Beecher's daughter Harriet later remembered the effect of all this on her father's mind: it kept him "at the white heat of enthusiasm." Impetuous and moody, often absentminded, his dress in habitual disarray, Beecher was an amiable eccentric who seemed always in motion. Stowe recalled that her father's various activities so excited him that often he had to work off excess energy. In his backyard, he kept "parallel bars, a single bar, ladder, and other simple gymnastic apparatus," where he would sometimes astonish his ministerial visitors by climbing ropes hand over hand, whirling over on the single bar, lifting weights, and performing other athletic feats. In inclement weather he moved to his cellar, where, she recalled, he kept a load of sand, "to which he would run at odd intervals and shovel vigorously," throwing it from one side of the room to the other![13] He was a force of nature who Unitarians had good reason to resent and fear.

In his *Autobiography*, Beecher described how each week new faces eager to hear his message appeared in his church, many of whom eventually joined his congregation. They "come on purpose to hear me," he wrote, "brought by curiosity or the invitation or influence of friends." Once in his church, they felt "an abatement of prejudice, and not infrequently surprise, approbation, solicitude, and ultimately conversion." Other Unitarians started to worry about such desertions and forbade their wives and daughters to attend his meetings. So much for the liberals' much-vaunted principles of toleration, Beecher sniffed. Even Baptists came to see what was going on, he gleefully recorded, and pretty soon they too "began to revive."[14]

Then, in 1830, Beecher's Hanover Street Church burned to the ground, an event fraught with significance. In addition to swelling crosscurrents of theology sweeping New England—Beecher versus the Unitarian upstarts, Harvard versus Yale, Andover versus Harvard—Boston suffered from simmering class tensions never far from the surface. The meetinghouse fire triggered open animosity between temperance reformers like Beecher and the laboring classes. Reportedly, Boston's fire companies, made up of workingmen who joined the companies for fraternal and bibulous reasons, did not even attempt to extinguish it. Instead, they loitered with other spectators who were taking in the sight, even joining in bawdy antitemperance songs.[15]

Among the many onlookers were Unitarians, many of whom jeered the spectacle. One of them, however, a young clergyman, was dismayed when he realized that some of his own congregation were among those celebrating the Hanover Street Church's loss. The following Sabbath he urged his parishioners to teach their children that, "if a fire consume a church that is not of your communion or name," the event did not "command" derision but instead "Christian sympathy."[16]

Not discouraged by the loss, Beecher remained in Boston, ministering to the Salem Street Church, in the city's North End, until his own church could reconstitute (they rebuilt on Bowdoin Street, on Beacon Hill). As this suggests, long gone was the dream of social harmony that had animated the early settlers of New England. Now, Boston, like most of New England, witnessed a proliferation of competing faiths. Society, even as its merchants made the city into one of the nation's most important commercial centers, was fractious, which made that young Unitarian minister's reaction to the fire all the more unusual. Given Beecher's persistent excoriation of Unitarianism as the source of contemporary spiritual decline, why didn't this fellow display the same scorn and jealousy as so many of his fellow Unitarians?

He was twenty-seven-year-old Ralph Waldo Emerson, whose church, Boston's Second, stood at the opposite end of Hanover Street. Although no one then knew it, soon enough this young man's influence rivaled and then surpassed Beecher's and even challenged that of Jonathan Edwards.

The Young Emerson

Emerson's lineage fit the mold of the new liberal Christians.[17] His father, William, was a staunch Federalist who supported a social order whose leadership lay in the professional and merchant elite, men of property and means. These good Federalists held to standards of republican virtue: loyal, Christian citizens who curtailed self-serving behavior for the good of the commonweal. They deplored the recent fragmentation of the American society into special interests, precisely the danger that the authors of the *Federalist Papers* tried to prevent. These included the newly emergent Jeffersonian Republicans, who directly challenged the Federalists, horrifying them with their deistical views; disruptive, competing religious groups, like the lower-class Universalists and Methodists; and in the secular realm, the laboring classes, who battled for improved workers' wages and hours.

As the reaction to the fire at the Hanover Street Church demonstrated, although Federalists yearned for order and stability in their personal and social relations, everywhere their ideals of order and harmony were under attack. In reaction, they became as obstreperous as any of the other competing groups whom they could no longer silence and who ignored their demands for deference to an older religious and social order. This made Emerson's sympathetic view of the Hanover Street Church fire even more unusual.

Emerson's father oversaw Boston's First Church until his untimely death in 1811. His profile fit the Federalists to a tee: an early leader of the liberal Christian movement, editor of their literary periodical, the *Monthly Anthology*, and a founder of such important cultural institutions as the Massachusetts Historical Society and the Boston Athenaeum. William Emerson took pride in having succeeded to the pulpit of Charles Chauncy, for he applauded his predecessor's condemnation of revivalism and the New Divinity. It seemed natural that his son would follow in his footsteps.

Ralph Waldo Emerson (he was called "Waldo") was born in Boston in 1803 into a family that eventually totaled five boys. At the age of nine he was enrolled at the Boston Latin School, where most boys of his social class prepared for college and then for a career in the ministry, law, medicine, or increasingly, the merchant trades. But before he could graduate from Boston Latin, his family's situation changed. His father's death in 1811 plunged the family into a genteel poverty so trying that his mother had to take in boarders and send off some of her boys to live with relatives in nearby towns. Waldo frequently ended up in Concord, where he lived with his grandfather, the Reverend Ezra Ripley, the town's venerable Unitarian minister; or in Maine with his aunt Mary Moody Emerson, the only member of the extended family who questioned the rest of the family's wholehearted embrace of liberal Christianity.

The competing factions of Protestant theology collided in the person and thoughts of Mary Moody Emerson.[18] Widely read, she was neither Calvinist, Arminian, Unitarian, or Romantic but a remarkable amalgam of all four. She frequently returned to Edwards's works. In 1810 in a set of "almanacks" or journals, which she shared from time to time with her nephew, she noted how she had grappled with Edwards's *Freedom of the Will.* She had taken another "glance at Edwards," she wrote one day, "and the moral virtue of atonement appeared before me under his influence." "Ah wonderful & joyous condition of any created being," she added, "whose destiny refers him to his Creator in the most absolute and unconditional dependence—that Creator the *first Cause* in the universe of every effect—the Alpha & Omega—the Origin of wisdom & goodness—how simple—how natural the reliance—the *branch* flourishes no longer than adhering to the *vine*."[19] *Freedom of the Will* stayed with her throughout her life.

In Concord the elderly Ezra Ripley prepared Emerson for Harvard College, again the logical choice for someone of his background. He entered in 1817 and graduated four years later, an unexceptional student whose reduced family circumstances marked him: because of his need for financial aid, he had to serve as "waiter" to the college's president, James Thornton Kirkland. After graduation, Emerson taught at his brother William's school for young ladies in Boston but soon realized that pedagogy was not his calling. He began study for the ministry with one of the foremost Unitarian clergymen, the Reverend William Ellery Channing of Boston's Federal Street Church, who in 1819 had openly named the liberal church movement he led "Unitarian Christianity" and who was a prime mover in many contemporary reform activities, including abolition.[20] In 1825 Emerson entered the Harvard Divinity School, in its "middle" class. Four years later, after more than a year of probationary preaching in other area churches, he was called to a prestigious position, Boston's Second Church.

During this same period, he met sixteen-year-old Ellen Tucker, to whom he was engaged in 1828. She came from a wealthy Boston commercial family and by all accounts was very attractive, with large, dark eyes and rich, thick hair. After her father's death, she lived with her mother and stepfather in Concord, New Hampshire, where she enjoyed the natural world, rode horses, and wrote poetry. She was head-over-heels in love with Waldo, their playful correspondence during the courtship full of pleasantries that indicate how smitten they both were. "I want to tell you that I love you very much and I would like to have you love me always," she wrote, playfully adding, "If consistent with your future plans."[21] Indeed, it was. She was a perfect match for Waldo, and in 1829, during the time when he was under consideration by the Second Church, they were married in New Hampshire with festivities that lasted three days. After he received his coveted position, they settled in Boston.

But the young Emerson soon fell out with his congregation over his belief that they were too wedded to ritual and not sufficiently receptive to the spiritual truths he proffered. One such rite was the administration, every other month, of the sacrament of the Lord's Supper. He found it had no practical effect on his people. Then, in 1831, even as he reconsidered his dedication to the sacrament, Ellen, only nineteen years old, died of tuberculosis. Emerson, himself only twenty-seven, was shattered. For over a year he walked to her tomb daily. In the spring of 1832, still grief-stricken, he literally opened her coffin, as though wanting to convince himself of death's reality and that she was indeed gone.

Through the summer, still in mourning, he pressed the issue of communion with a committee of the church's leaders, stating his wish to discontinue the practice. They deliberated but decided to maintain the communion table. Emerson was not mollified. On September 9 he dramatically brought his reservations before the entire congregation in a sermon, "The Lord's Supper," on a text from Paul's letter to the Romans 14:17: "The Kingdom of God is not meat and drink; but righteousness and peace, and joy in the Holy Ghost."

"Most men find the bread and wine no aid to devotion, and to some it is a painful impediment," he declared. "To eat bread is one thing," he told his flock; "to love the precepts of Christ and resolve to obey them is another." Finding his congregation still unmoved by his arguments, Emerson declared, "this mode of commemorating Christ is not suitable to me. That is reason enough why I should abandon it."[22] It was his final sermon there.

The painful, drawn-out affair was finally over, but it had taken a lot from Emerson, emotionally and physically. Through it all he suffered from such severe diarrhea that, he wrote his aunt, it had "stripped [him] to the bones." He felt like a "wasted, peevish invalid."[23] In midwinter 1833, his ministry at the Second Church behind him and his personal life in tatters, he made plans to sail for Europe to recuperate.

Transcendentalism

While studying for the ministry, Emerson had been introduced to new currents of European philosophy and theology that were washing up on America's shores. He first encountered these through his interest in scriptural exegesis, "the Higher Criticism" of the Bible that was marked by detailed contextual and philological analysis, and exemplified by the scholarship of Johann Gottfried von Herder, Johann Gottfried Eichhorn, and Johann Jakob Griesbach.[24] Emerson's immersion in their works had helped him shape his arguments about the Lord's Supper.

Soon, Emerson began to move away from the strict empiricism of philosophers like John Locke and his descendants in the "Common Sense" school and gravitated to German idealism. Some others of the younger liberal clergy welcomed the revolution wrought by Immanuel Kant, Johann Gottlieb Fichte, and others who championed the inherent powers of the human mind, unlike Locke and his followers, who believed that external circumstances formed the basis of mental concepts, a position that older Unitarians still stubbornly maintained. The arrival in the United States of European Romantic ideas opened new ways to understand the self and its relation to the universe and pushed many young clergy to a more radical position that their Trinitarian and Unitarian opponents would later call "transcendentalist."[25]

No fixed creed marked membership in this group, even though for a while in the mid-1830s a dozen or so met informally as the Symposium or Transcendental Club. One near contemporary noted that they were liberal thinkers who agreed on "nothing but their liberality." He qualified his assessment by quoting the Reverend James Freeman Clarke, another Unitarian minister and transcendentalist fellow traveler, who wryly noted that "they call themselves 'the club of the like-minded,'" primarily because "no two . . . thought alike." One of them, Frederic Henry Hedge, recalled, "the only guest not welcome was intolerance."[26]

By siding with the Germans against empiricism, transcendentalists came to perceive the world in new ways. Individual consciousness rather than external stimuli was the key. They maintained that peoples' ideas do not come through the five senses, or the powers of reasoning, as Locke believed, but as one of their fellow travelers put it, are "either the result of direct revelation from God, his immediate inspiration, or his immanent presence in the spiritual world." Charles Mayo Ellis continued, the doctrine of transcendentalism implies "the substantive, independent existence of the soul of man, the reality of conscience, the religious sense, the inner light, of man's religious affections, his knowledge of right and truth, his sense of duty" as well as his love for beauty and holiness. None of these were dependent on external stimuli nor "on education, custom, command, or anything beyond man himself."[27]

According to Ellis, the opposing worldview, in which man derived all ideas from external stimuli, led "to atheism, to a religion that is but self-interest—an ethical code which makes right synonymous with indulgence of appetite, justice one with expediency and reduces our love of what is good, beautiful, true and divine, to habit, association, or interest." Transcendentalists did not concern themselves with such things as the divine origin of Sabbath, the "authenticity or authority of the old or new testaments, their infallible or plenary inspiration," or the "trinity or unity, the humanity or divinity of the Saviour," questions that for years fueled debates between Unitarians and their more conservative Trinitarian brethren.[28] Instead, they focused on the universal presence of the spiritual element in mankind. Within each individual, they maintained, is a spiritual principle that supersedes outward laws or injunctions and that allows one to distinguish between good and evil.

The "like-minded" had discovered a novel body of European ideas through which they could understand and address their religious dissatisfaction. A notion of such universal divine inspiration—grace as the birthright of all—was the bedrock of this new movement that was gaining notice in the early 1830s just as Emerson was reconsidering his commitment to the ministry. It was left to him to ascertain the practical implications of this liberating premise, the spiritual equivalent of the democratic ideal that all men are created equal. What would a secular order based on these premises resemble?

Europe

Before Emerson addressed that question, he had to face the consequences of his resignation from the ministry. The profession had offered him a career of thought and action that extended into a "dazzling infinity" as he pondered the moral significance of human life. "To make the soul, aforetime the servant of the senses, acquainted with the secret of its own power" and "to teach man that by self-renouncement a heaven of which he had no conception, begins at once in his heart"—was this not the noblest vocation?[29] But how could he do this now that he had resigned? He had to find another way to reveal to men and women that they were sons and daughters of God.

Emerson mulled over his vocation on his European journey. He had felt a powerful need to get away. On top of the pressures that came with his resignation, he was devastated by the loss of Ellen. From James Marsh, a professor at the University of Vermont who had arranged for the American publication of some of Samuel Taylor Coleridge's writings, he learned that obedience to the law within (the Reason) is central to a virtuous life and that the human mind is the source of order in the universe. Now, he began to consider the relation of nature to spirit, particularly how God had made nature so orderly and harmonious that it mirrored the spiritual realm. With his beloved Ellen in the grave, Emerson's understanding of salvation pivoted on the perception of the relation between man and the whole.

To understand this was to unravel the mystery of how people might attain social harmony. If man consulted one's individual conscience to direct moral behavior, rather than relying on social convention or outward law, one would see that abandoning private interest, one's selfishness, was central to establishing a new social order. "My neighbor," Emerson confided, "feels the wrong that my self-interest produces, feels that here is appropriation, here is not love, and shrinks from me as far as I have shrunk from him."[30] It was time to challenge this isolation and alienation, and to return humanity to a more harmonious, organic state that mirrored God's laws, even as it preserved the inherent dignity of each individual.

In late December 1832 Emerson booked a passage on a ship leaving for the Mediterranean. In early February he visited Malta, and then Sicily, Italy, and France. In Italy he went to Naples and then Rome, where he heard the Pope's sermon on Easter Sunday; and to Florence, visiting sites and monuments about which he had read since his youth. Next, he crossed the mountains to Switzerland and made his way to Paris. He visited the Louvre, the King's Library, and various Parisian reading rooms, filled with newspapers and journals he had never encountered. Then in July, he found himself in the Jardin des Plantes, which before the French Revolution had been called the King's Garden.

The visit was transformative. The Jardin des Plantes was more than a botanical garden. It was a major scientific research center where the main project was to classify all plant life from living specimens. The exhibits were laid out according to the reigning Linnaean classification system, and this illustration of the connections among various, seemingly different, species transfixed Emerson. There were comparable collections of bird and animal specimens, insects and minerals, displayed in such a way as to indicate the development of cognate or new species and forms. Emerson was impressed by "the inexhaustible riches of nature," for here he saw that "the Universe is a more amazing puzzle than ever." Pondering the highly organized and well-presented exhibits, he saw more clearly man's place in the natural world. Later, he wrote in his journal that at the collections, "I feel the centipede in me—cayman, carp, eagle, and fox." "I am moved by strange sympathies," he continued. "I say continually, I will be a naturalist."[31] A few days later, this memorable visit now uppermost in his mind, he left for England.

There, he made it his business to meet the chief literary men. In August he visited Coleridge at Highgate. The poet was now sixty-one years old, a "short thick old man with bright blue eyes" and a "great snuff taker" who quickly "soiled his cravat & neat black suit." Although Emerson was totally unknown to him and Emerson's visit unannounced, Coleridge gave him an hour of his time. He talked *at* Emerson virtually nonstop, most of the time criticizing Unitarianism and William Ellery Channing, whom he had met. Coleridge regretted that Channing remained loyal to the Unitarian faith. He had once been a Unitarian himself, Coleridge told his young visitor, and thus "knew what quackery it was." Emerson countered by insisting that many American Unitarians read Coleridge's books "with pleasure," even if they did not subscribe to his philosophy.[32]

Emerson then crossed to Scotland and visited Thomas Carlyle, a brilliant essayist who at thirty-seven had done almost as much as Coleridge to make English speakers familiar with German idealist philosophy. Emerson had learned Carlyle's name only on reaching Europe, but he had read approvingly some of his anonymously published essays on Fichte and Kant in the *Edinburgh Review*. Carlyle and his charismatic wife, Jane, persuaded Emerson to stay overnight, and they talked for hours on many topics, including contemporary social problems. The two men became fast friends and maintained a correspondence that lasted throughout Carlyle's lifetime.

Next, Emerson dropped in on William Wordsworth. The great poet was sixty-three and already quite feeble, "a plain looking elderly man in goggles" who talked "with great simplicity." Unlike Coleridge, Wordsworth spoke warmly of Channing but criticized Carlyle, whom he termed "insane" and "defied the sympathies of everyone." He also made clear his dislike for much of the new German thought. Goethe's *Wilhelm Meister's Apprenticeship*, Wordsworth opined, was "like flies crossing each other in the air" and all "fornication." Regardless, Emerson enjoyed the visit and found his host's egotism not at all displeasing.[33] With each luminary on his list now checked off, Emerson traveled from the Lake Country to Liverpool, where he boarded a ship for the United States. He had been gone nine months, and he was rested, invigorated, transformed.

Shortly after his arrival in Boston and needing income, Emerson turned to lecturing. When asked to speak at the newly established Boston Society of Natural History, he quickly agreed. The topic he suggested, "The Uses of Natural History," meshed perfectly with his recent experience in Europe. In November 1833 his audience essentially heard an early draft of the epochal book that he would publish three years later.

As the title of his lecture indicates, Emerson outlined various uses that might come from the study of nature. The activity was healthy, bringing people outdoors, and useful, for it served man for his food, shelter, and other needs. Such study of nature also delighted man as he contemplated its pervasive order and fitness. It disciplined the mind, making him understand the need for the kind of close observation that so rewarded the naturalist. Finally, Emerson observed, science "explain[ed] man to himself," for with "the knowledge of all the facts and all the laws of nature" at his fingertips, he would see "his true place in the system of beings." Emerson reminded his audience that nature was the source of man's language and metaphors, that "correspondence of the outward world to the inward world of thought and emotions." Thinking of his experience in Paris, he concluded, "Nature is a language and every new fact one learns is a new word." "I wish to learn this language," he told the assembly, "not that I may know a new grammar, but that I may read the great book which is written in that tongue."[34]

His lecture a success, Emerson was soon asked to prepare an entire series on the subject. The city's Mechanics Institute also commissioned him to speak on other, related topics: "Science," "Italy," "English Literature," and "Human Culture." He began to realize that the lyceum circuit, as the recent popularity of public lecturing was termed, offered the springboard he sought. It provided venues from which to preach the spirit in a new way, not as clergyman or scientist but as a moral philosopher who reflected on the relation between man, nature, and the spirit.

In the early summer of 1836 Emerson wrote his brother William, "My little book is almost done." "Its title is *Nature*," he continued. "My design is to follow it with another essay, *Spirit*, and the two shall make a decent volume."[35] He never wrote the second part, perhaps realizing that he had accomplished what he sought in the penultimate chapter of *Nature* called, simply, "Spirit."[36] *Nature* was his first contribution to the emergent discourse of transcendentalism, albeit several years after Orestes Brownson, George Ripley, and Frederic Henry Hedge had made their debuts in print with lengthy essays in which they had announced allegiance to European idealism as well as to programs of radical social reform.

Emerson was less well versed in German philosophy than these others. His idealism originated in a long-standing interest in Coleridge and Carlyle, in Plato and eighteenth-century Neoplatonism, and in Boston apothecary Sampson Reed's redaction of Emanuel Swedenborg's account of the correspondence between the natural and spiritual worlds, a book that Emerson praised as "the best thing since Plato of Plato's kind."[37] Brownson and Ripley had already read the Germans in the original, despite coming to transcendentalism by a different route, one that diverged in some ways from Emerson's.

His temperamental difference from many of his peers did not go unnoticed. When Brownson reviewed *Nature* in the *Boston Reformer*, he noted presciently that the book was "aesthetical rather than philosophical." In the *United States Magazine and Democratic Review*, Elizabeth Peabody, one of the most prominent women transcendentalists, agreed. "We have said that 'Nature' is a poem; but it is written in prose." But Emerson's aphoristic style offended some reviewers. Unitarian Francis Bowen, in the *Christian Examiner*, noted that, although there was much of worth in Emerson's book, its effect was "injured by occasional vagueness of expression, and by a vein of mysticism that pervades the writer's whole course of thought," so much so that the book "produced the impression of a disordered dream."[38]

What did Emerson intend with this book, published anonymously in a run of five hundred copies? When he sent Carlyle a copy within a week of publication, he described it self-deprecatingly as "an entering wedge," he hoped, for something worthier and more significant.[39] In it he deployed philosophical idealism to open peoples' eyes to their spiritual inheritance. Hence his pervasive metaphors of sight and blindness, which achieved their most memorable expression in the "transparent eye-ball" passage in the book's opening pages. There Emerson described the merger of the "Me" and the "Not-Me" (terms Carlyle had used in *Sartor Resartus* and that he had in turn taken from the German philosopher Jakob Friedrich Fries) in an ecstatic experience: "Standing on the bare ground,—my head bathed by the blithe air, and uplifted into infinite space,—all mean egotism vanishes. I become a transparent eye-ball; I am nothing; I see all; the currents of the Universal Being circulate through me; I am part or particle of God."[40]

The metaphor of sight was present from the book's first line. "Our age is retrospective," he began. While "the foregoing generations beheld God and nature face to face," rather than having "an original relation to the universe," contemporaries saw "through their eyes." As a result, man lived in a fallen world, and the "the ruin or blank" that he saw when he looked around him was in his "own eye." Fittingly, the book ends with a section called "prospects"—a looking forward—and, in the very last line, with the promise that, if man views nature rightly, he will inhabit a new world, which "he shall enter without more wonder than the blind man feels who is gradually restored to perfect sight."[41]

Emerson Ascendant

Emerson was one of several Unitarians ministers who had reconsidered their vocation because of their readings in the new European thought. He was no longer just responding to denominational controversies but rather to his sense that the world had become an unsettled, troubled place that needed significant reformation. Politically, economically, and socially, it was changing in ways that betrayed the noble vision of the Founding Fathers. Americans' sense of time, distance, and permanence had been forever changed with the development of railroads and steamboats, telegraphs and photographs. Industrialization had transformed the meaning of work. It had become "labor," and attendant on it was not only a host of problems over wages, work hours, and an increasing distance between labor and capital but also a new thing called "leisure," time liberated from labor that could be used in new ways. It was indeed a brave new world, and the transcendentalists confronted it head-on.

Emerson's cousin George Ripley formulated plans that came to fruition in 1841 at his utopian community, Brook Farm, in nearby West Roxbury. Orestes Brownson, true to his lower-class upbringing, found his calling in the cause of the worker, championing a more equitable wage labor. Theodore Parker, eventually ostracized by the area's Unitarians for his radical religious views, soon started his own nondenominational church in Boston; it grew to such size that it finally occupied the Melodeon, one of the city's largest halls. He also was a fervent abolitionist and one of John Brown's "Secret Six," conspirators in his ragtag attack on Harper's Ferry in 1859. Frederic Henry Hedge, one of the few transcendentalists who had read the German philosophers in the original, remained pastor of a Unitarian congregation in Bangor, Maine.

Brownson was one of the few transcendentalists without a college education. Born to a poor farming family in Vermont, he moved through several denominations until he heard Channing preach and knocked at Unitarianism's door.[42] For a while, he supported Frances "Fanny" Wright and Robert Dale Owen's Working Men's Party, all the while reading avidly in French socialist thought, particularly the works of Claude Henri de Saint-Simon.[43] Settling in the Boston area, he earned respect for his views and reform activities and soon enough became minister at large to the city's poor. He continued to read widely, now in German thought, and championed the laboring classes.

In 1836 Brownson was a clergyman who believed that the conflict between labor and capital prevented any lasting social harmony. He wanted to provide the working man with the education and ministry he needed to better his lot and thus provide the sociability so sorely missing. His *New Views of Christianity, Society, and the Church* appeared the same year as *Nature* and introduced a powerful, new voice for social reform. Therein he thundered that Christians had to raise a universal cry against "the frigid utilitarianism of the last century," its "money-getting" and "desire for worldly wealth and renown." Everywhere, people cared about material things, but the new church he sought to institute would reconcile matter with Spirit. Solidarity with the worker was essential: "PROGRESS is our law and our first step is UNION."[44]

Unsurprisingly, early on his path crossed that of George Ripley, and the young Unitarian clergyman was impressed. Ripley grew up in a merchant's family in Greenfield, Massachusetts, and like his cousin Emerson he had attended Harvard.[45] He was ordained over a small congregation of the "middling" sort in Boston and soon began to read widely in French and German philosophy and theology, as his new friend Brownson was doing. In his weekly sermons Ripley preached a belief in a universal, internal religious principle that validated faith and united all men and women.

Acting on this principle, in 1841 he left his pulpit to start Brook Farm, a cooperative community just outside of Boston. This utopian enterprise, which lasted six years and was one of several-score such experiments throughout the country, was dedicated to the proposition that the intellectual and the worker deserved the same pay and benefits. At Brook Farm, both would flourish and influence each other as all members rotated through necessary tasks in this agricultural and artisanal enterprise: they raised dairy cows, made window sashes, and started pottery and other workshops. All members also participated in such educational activities as lectures, musical performances, and plays.[46]

Brownson and Ripley became great friends—"I loved him as I loved no other man," Brownson later wrote—and both became the field generals of the emergent transcendentalist movement, popularizing idealist thought through seminal publications and theorizing how to apply it to pressing social needs.[47] They took transcendentalist ideas in a very different direction from Emerson: not hoping for the promotion of individual self-culture as much as for the reformation of a crass, materialistic, and spiritually bereft American polity.

Transcendental idealism, however, led Emerson in a different direction. He believed that social harmony was possible only if each individual was empowered by belief in himself as "part or particle of God," and he had little patience with collective social activism. He valued spiritual growth and self-expression, themes he developed on the lecture circuit in the late 1830s. Introspection and self-reliance were central to him. Brownson, Ripley, and soon enough, Theodore Parker stressed the brotherhood of man and outer-directed behavior for the common good, an ethic inherited in part from a mixture of Edwardsean theology and the civic republicanism of the post-Revolutionary period, also inflected by contemporary European socialism.

Emerson thought that his fellow transcendentalists wasted their time and talent in quixotic ventures. He criticized them explicitly in a lecture on "New England Reformers" delivered in Boston early in 1844. In their haste to do away with the old, he observed, reformers often did not adequately prepare to affirm and construct something in its place. To focus on one moral evil—say, intemperance—elided the fact that "the wave of evil washes all our institutions alike," so that one could not afford to spend time on such selective attacks. Equally problematic was many reformers' increasing reliance on "association" (a term borrowed from the French utopian socialist Charles Fourier) to combat social injustice. Friendship and association were fine, Emerson thought, so long as one realized that "no society can ever be so large as one man."[48] In relying too much on others, a person never became fully empowered.

Only after an individual has experienced the paradise within, Emerson believed, should he join with others, presumably similarly enlightened, to restore paradise without. Only then can institutions, comprised as they are of discrete individuals, change. Admittedly, men and women at work together appear to accomplish more than individuals working at discrete tasks. But any reform resulting from such efforts remained cosmetic unless there was an inward "union." Reform cannot be realized merely by some covenant, for those who band together in an imperfect state are, on all sides, "cramped and diminished" in proportion. "The union," he concluded, "must be ideal in actual individualism."[49]

Emerson's journals following his European trip show him thinking through his epiphany in the Jardin des Plantes and considering the interconnectedness of nature's myriad parts. Few had recognized the significance of this fact. "The Idea according to which the Universe is made is wholly wanting to us; is it not?" he asked. He believed now that the material world was merely the expression of the spiritual world and that "there is imparted to every man the Divine light of Reason sufficient not only to plant corn & grind wheat by but also to illuminate all his life his social, political, religious actions." He began to discern the political implications of his newly acquired faith. "/Democracy/Freedom/ has its root," he wrote, "in the Sacred truth that every man hath in him the divine Reason or that though few men since the creation of the world live according to the dictates of Reason, yet all men are created capable of so doing." Herein "is the equality & the only equality of all men."[50]

Emerson articulated these beliefs powerfully in the next two books he published, *Essays* (1841) and *Essays: Second Series* (1844), but he had prepared for these interventions a few years earlier. The year after *Nature*, he gave a stirring Phi Beta Kappa address, entitled "The American Scholar," to Harvard's class of 1837, and the next year he started a theological pamphlet war with a fiery address to the graduating class of the Harvard Divinity School. There, after reading *Nature*, whose authorship now was an open secret, several of the graduates had invited him to speak.

Emerson had urged young Harvard graduates to experience and act in the world, and he repeated this advice to the theological students. He excoriated contemporary clergy for their inability to preach from their own personal experiences. He recounted his own disappointment in a local minister who had sorely tempted him to stop attending services. One day in meeting, "a snow storm was falling all around us," he explained, and while it was real, the preacher was "merely spectral." "The eye felt the sad contrast in looking at him," Emerson continued, "and then out of the window behind him, into the beautiful meteor of the snow." Sadly, this clergyman had never spoken "one word that intimated that he had laughed or wept, was married or in love, had been commended, or cheated, or chagrined." He had failed dismally at "the capital secret" of his profession, to "convert life into truth."[51]

In that address, Emerson declared that every man and woman was as divine as Christ, a shocking proposition to deliver in front of his former professors. Jesus, Emerson declared, belonged to the true race of prophets because "he saw with open eye the mystery of the soul." He recognized the symbiotic relationship of matter and spirit and understood his divinity in and through it (as a transcendentalist did). Alone in all history, Emerson claimed, Christ estimated humanity's greatness, for he saw that God incarnates himself in man. "'I am divine,'" Christ said. "'Through me, God acts; through me, speaks. Would you see God, see me; or see thee, when thou also thinkest as I now think.'" Christ's message was that all men and women are divine and have to be awakened to this fact. This was the purpose of his teachings. But shortly after Christ's death, his followers distorted his memory and doctrine. They mistook the "idioms" of his language and the "figures of his rhetoric" for truth and built their churches "on his tropes" rather than on his principles.[52]

In the six years between the publication of the "Divinity School Address," which caused a great commotion in Boston's religious circles, and the appearance of *Essays: Second Series*, Emerson moved from being a little-known lightning rod for the movement's religious and philosophical eccentricity to center stage as its chief proselytizer of an imperial self. By the 1840s, enthusiastic applause for Emerson drowned dissident voices. His understanding of transcendentalism began—first in New England, then in the old Northwest and Middle Atlantic states, and eventually across the continent—to engender an almost mystical belief in the divine power of the individual to direct his own life. What did Emerson say and how did he say it, so that Americans came to view him as one of democracy's chief spokespersons? And what kind of society did he envision if men and women realized the promise of such individual empowerment as all recognized their Christ-like divinity?

Emerson the Essayist

In 1834 when he was lecturing in New Bedford, Massachusetts, a young woman by the name of Lidian Jackson was enthralled by his performance, reportedly not moving a muscle throughout. The lecturer's ideas echoed many of her own. She loved poetry and read Goethe in German. With her long, uncut hair and plain face, she was not as attractive as Ellen, but her temperament—she had strong emotions and a love of animals and nature—fit Emerson's needs at this crucial time, and the two courted and soon married. Lidian was more traditionally religious than her husband, having experienced conversion as a young woman and later become a devotee of seances and spiritualism in general. They were married when he was thirty and she thirty-one, and she remained his trusted helpmeet and supporter throughout his life. Lidian, whom Emerson playfully called "Mine Asia" because of his love of Eastern literature (she always referred to him as "Mr. Emerson"), was exactly who he needed.

To support his family between 1836 and 1838—he now had two children—Emerson gave two series of lectures in Boston, a total of twenty-two offerings, on "The Philosophy of History." Late in 1838 he followed with another, on "Human Culture," and the next season he discussed "The Present Age," an assessment of the state of social and cultural reform. Often repeated at least in part in other New England communities, these talks afforded him a degree of publicity, as well as substantial income, which when added to the inheritance he had received after Ellen's death, afforded him a comfortable life.

Particularly in Boston, the public vied for tickets and invitations to the convivial receptions that often closed the evening's presentations. Most of all, they sought to mingle with the magnetic Emerson. Six feet tall, with a long neck and sloping shoulders, he had dark brown hair, piercing blue eyes, and a Roman nose, his most prominent feature. He seemed oracular, revealing truth in finely chiseled sentences, each of which might be infinitely expanded but that he treated instead like fragments of an artfully constructed mosaic. He punctuated his sentences by clenching his fist, knuckles up, arm bent at the elbow, only to deliver a downward blow with this forearm to emphasize what he considered most important. His friend Margaret Fuller recalled that his voice was "full and sweet rather than sonorous, yet flexible, and haunted by many modulations, as even instruments of wood or brass become after they have been long played on with skill and taste."[53] One went to *listen* to Emerson, not to be entertained. If not all in attendance captured his full meaning, they believed they were in the presence of genius.

In the early summer of 1839 Emerson decided to go through his ample manuscripts—he had six volumes of sermons and lectures and scores of journals—and select material for his first substantial book. He worked mainly from the journals, which he had begun indexing around certain chief topics, settling quickly on "History" and "Self-Reliance." His volume, *Essays*, published in 1841, was composed of twelve essays, including "Compensation," "Spiritual Laws," "Circles," and "The Over-Soul." But the pivotal essay was "Self-Reliance," in which he praised the individual who learns "to detect and watch that gleam of light which flashes across the mind from within."

Emerson described self-reliance as nothing less than a willingness to "believe that what is true for you in your private heart is true for all men." Over time, as mankind became increasingly entangled in social bonds and the selfishness that too often tightened them, this inner voice had grown "faint and inaudible." One had to regain access to this reservoir of spirituality and proclaim self-sufficiency. "Trust thyself," he counseled. "Every heart vibrates to that iron string."[54]

As he had said in *Nature* and *The American Scholar*, Emerson urged that access to this intuition came from living fully in the present, not by regretting the past or anticipating the future. Only then does one realize that a greater self-reliance will "work a revolution in all the offices and relations of men; in their religion; in their education; in their pursuits; their modes of living; their association; in their property; in their speculative views." In other words, self-reliance would initiate a nineteenth-century version of those glorious times for which Edwards and earlier generations had prayed. Let reformers summon "conventions and vote and resolve in multitude." Such actions were bound to fail because God "deigns to enter and inhabit you" by "a method precisely the reverse." When one asserts one's "Will," Emerson continued, one binds "the wheel of Chance" and is free from worry over its revolutions.[55]

"In all my lectures," he once opined, "I have taught one doctrine: the infinitude of the private man." So, unsurprisingly, the other essays in the collection reinforced this idea.[56] In "The Oversoul" Emerson spoke of that divine current, "that Unity . . . within which every man's particular being is contained and made one with all others," and that flows through intuition to inform one's morality. In a comment Edwards might have uttered, he explained that one distinguishes "the announcements of the soul" by the term "*Revelation*," for "an influx of the Divine mind into our mind." In such communications "the power to see is not separated from the will to do." Let one learn, Emerson urged, "the revelation of all nature and all thought . . . that the Highest dwells within him."[57]

And what of the everywhere-visible inequalities of wealth and condition that Brownson and Ripley sought to remedy? If one viewed the facts clearly, Emerson declared, such things would not matter, for "Love reduces them as the sun melts the iceberg in the sea." "The heart and soul of all men being one," he declared, "this bitterness of *His* and *Mine* ceases."[58]

Emerson's collection of essays provided a troubled world a way to cope with attendant change and confusion. It also presumed a society open enough to tolerate those who went against its precepts and expectations as they followed their consciences. On the lecture platform and in the press, Emerson forged tools through which Americans could understand and shape their novel condition, neither resisting nor condemning it, but having the self-confidence to recognize that all was for the good, even if the majority of their peers did not think so. And if the circumstances of life still seemed overwhelming, the solution was yet more self-confidence.

Essays: Second Series, which he published three years later, was qualitatively different, the work of an optimist whom experience has chastened. Early in 1842 Emerson was mourning the death of John Thoreau, Henry's older brother and a beloved schoolmaster in the community, who had died of tetanus after an accidental cut from his razor. Then, to the whole town of Concord's horror, within days Emerson also lost his much-loved five-year-old son, Waldo, to scarlet fever.

The child was the favorite of many in the Concord community, especially of Emerson's acolyte Henry David Thoreau, who had him help build a toy house for Waldo's sister, Ellen. Waldo was Emerson's constant companion: he often played in the study where Emerson worked and slept in a trundle bed in his parents' room. He was a beautiful child, with dark, slicked down hair and expressive eyebrows. He loved his sibling, Ellen, two-and a-half years younger, and told his mother that he often prayed "that Ellen might live and grow up."

Early in January 1842 he contracted the fever and died three days later, even as his sister also struggled with the disease. Ellen survived, but Waldo's death shocked all who knew Emerson. Louisa May Alcott, a nine-year-old neighbor, came to the Emerson home the next morning to ask how the boy was. She recalled, "his father came to me, so worn with watching and changed by sorrow that I was startled and could only stammer out my message." "Child," Emerson replied, "he is dead." "That," she wrote, "was my first glimpse of a great grief."[59]

As shocking as was this loss, Emerson did not lose his faith in man's resilience. Buffeted by tragedy, he returned to—even doubled down on—his beliefs, to reconsider and refine how one might find the courage to go on in a world that too often was at cross-purposes to what he most desired. Nowhere was this more visible than in the remarkable essay "Experience," in which Emerson openly addressed the tragedy of his young son's death. Here he offered a different, more sobering view of man's struggle for self-reliance in a sometimes hostile universe.

"Experience" appears early in the volume, and it marks Emerson's mature understanding of the delicate relationship between an individual's "power" and "universal form," the way things are. In the epigram to the essay, he names the "lords of life" that he will subsequently elucidate, those inescapable facts that bind us as we struggle to make sense of our lives. What can humanity do with, or against, them?

The essay opens by describing humanity in a state of confusion. "Where are we?" Emerson asks. "We wake and find ourselves on a stair; there are stairs below us, which we seem to have ascended; there are stairs above us, many a one, which go upward and out of sight." But we cannot locate ourselves, because "sleep lingers all our lifetime about our eyes," making "all things swim and glitter." Gone is the piercing clarity of the "transparent eye-ball," that profound sense of merger with oversoul. Things are blurry, opaque, not transparent. "I take this evanescence and lubricity of all objects," Emerson continued, "to be the most unhandsome part of our condition."[60]

So, what is one to do in a world that is constantly shifting beneath, denying any purchase to move it the way one wishes? Meet life head-on, Emerson counseled; do not shirk the challenges that the "lords of life" present. "I am thankful for small mercies," Emerson writes. "To fill the hour,—that is happiness; to fill the hour and leave no crevice for a repentance or an approval." This, from the man who eight years earlier had urged each individual to build one's own world! Now, "to finish the moment, to find the journey's end in every step of the road, to live the greatest number of god hours, is wisdom." Self-consciousness, the center and glory of *Nature* and "Self-Reliance," now is regarded as mankind's bane, for the discovery we make that we exist is nothing less than "the Fall of Man."[61]

Personal tragedies were the main stimulus to these new thoughts but so too were contemporary circumstances of a different scale. The 1840s were the years of the rise of modern politicking between Democrats and Whigs that made elections resemble as much partisan brawls as the results of deliberative democracy; when southerners used Mexico's instability as a pretext for initiating a war that eventually increased the number of slave states; and when, as a result of this huge annexation, the national sin of slavery came ever closer to tearing apart the nation.

The nation's financial situation was no better. Following President Andrew Jackson's dismantling of the Bank of the United States and the Panic of 1837, the nation's first major depression, the economy was in disarray and poverty increasingly common.[62] What was there to feel good about if one took an honest look at the great American experiment in democracy? What could hold together such fraying bonds? Although Emerson at this point was not deeply involved in national politics, "Experience" showed that he would not give up on the promise of individual self-worth.

This was a new and wiser Emerson, for, as he noted, he was not "the novice [he] was fourteen, nor yet seven years ago." When people asked why he could not realize his world in the way he once had described, he turned from the question and simply urged "patience and patience," for "we shall win at last." We till our gardens, he explained. We eat our dinners, discuss household chores with our spouses, and think nothing of such things, while in fact we should savor them. "Never mind the ridicule, never mind the defeat," he concluded. "Up again old heart!"[63] His optimism soon enough butted up against even greater challenges, as the nation grew more divided and secession loomed.

Here Emerson's essay "Politics" demands attention, for it is essential to his understanding of the sovereign individual's obligation to the state. Predictably, he was suspicious of any organized activity that did not emphasize the importance of each individual's efforts. Republics, Emerson wrote, "abound in young civilians who believe that laws make the city," but the "wise know that foolish legislation is a rope of sand which perishes in the twisting."[64] The state, he urged, must follow and not co-opt the citizen's wish. Contemporary politics, he explained, existed for two reasons: to protect the citizen and to protect property. But while an individual can fare well in a system in which all have equal rights, property owners' social ranks obviously depend on how much of it they own. He wondered whether the nation's laws gave too much weight to the laws of property and suggested that the state's first consideration should remain the protection of individual rights.

As two-party politicking took definitive shape in the famous "Log Cabin and Hard Cider" campaign—the 1840 presidential contest that pitted Democrat Martin Van Buren against the Whig man of the people William Henry Harrison—Emerson lamented the partisan spirit that such contests engendered and encouraged. The "current radical party," the Democrats, which had inherited the Jacksonians' distrust of big government, was "destructive and aimless," with "no ulterior and divine ends," and operated only from hatred and selfishness. On the other side, the Whigs, the "conservative party," were composed of those who Emerson believed were the "moderate, able, and cultivated" part of the population, but who were only interested in support for the propertied classes.

He lamented that politics as a whole do not "build, nor write, nor cherish the arts, nor foster religion, nor establish schools, nor encourage science, nor emancipate the slave, nor befriend the poor, or the Indian, or the immigrant." The basis for the formation of the proper government in the log cabin and hard cider campaign should be "the will of the wise man, he who follows his higher law" and thus shows concern for the very subjects now ignored. Hence, Emerson concluded, "the less government we have the better." The antidote to the abuse of formal government was the influence of private character, the moral growth of the individual.[65] The universal appearance of such character would make the state unnecessary, for when men are governed by the Spirit, society can be maintained without the kinds of artificial restraints that so trammeled his contemporaries.

During the 1850s Emerson worked up a series of lectures on "The Conduct of Life," which he published under that title in 1860, on the cusp of the Civil War. He had signaled his serious engagement with abolition in 1844 when he spoke to the women of Concord at their annual celebration of the emancipation of the British West Indies, an address in which he also criticized his countrymen for their obsession with the market, which fueled the slave trade. When some of his townsmen found out what he intended to say on the topic, they refused to allow him to speak in any of Concord's churches. The sponsoring group of women settled on the courthouse, and when opponents of the event refused to ring the building's bell to summon townspeople, as was the custom, Emerson's young neighbor and acolyte Henry Thoreau took it upon himself to do just that. "We peddle," Emerson observed. "We truck, we sail, we row, we ride in cars, we creep in teams, we go in canals—to market, for the sale of goods." "The civility of no race can be perfect whilst another race is degraded," he wrote. "It is a doctrine of the oldest, and of the newest philosophy," he reminded his audience. "Man is one, and that you cannot injure any member, without a sympathetic injury to all members."[66]

This address saw a turn in Emerson's former reluctance to speak to contemporary politics, and in particular to devote himself first to the antislavery cause and then, beginning in 1846, to opposition to President James K. Polk's prosecution of the Mexican-American War and annexation of Texas. In the 1850s he was everywhere on the lecture platform urging support for abolition.[67]

He took particular umbrage at Massachusetts senator Daniel Webster's capitulation to the proslavery advocates when he supported the so-called Compromise of 1850, which included the infamous Fugitive Slave Law, which allowed slaveowners to reclaim slaves living in free states, action that "has forced all of us into politics." Webster's fame ended in this "filthy law," he thundered, now that he had become the "head of the slavery party in this country." "The word *liberty* in the mouth of Mr Webster," Emerson wrote irately in his journal, "sounds like the word love in the *mouth* of a courtesan."[68] Worse yet was the Kansas-Nebraska Bill of 1854, which nullified the Missouri Compromise of 1820, allowing for slavery north of the Mason-Dixon Line in those two new territories. In a speech in New York City, shortly following the passage of this bill, Emerson delivered another acerbic attack on the government's recent actions.

All these and other recent events gave his antislavery lectures and the essays in *The Conduct of Life* a particular effectiveness and power, and as well indicate an important shift in Emerson's championing of self-reliance. Instead, he began to emphasize the importance of character, one's ability to perform ethical actions for the good of one's fellow citizens. He addresses such topics such as "Fate," "Power," "Wealth," "Culture," "Behavior," "Worship," "Beauty," and "Illusions." Of these, the first, "Fate," best displays Emerson's continuing engagement with certain ideas about freedom that he had been investigating from *Nature* on and had recast so profoundly in "Experience." He understood that the moral order is best understood as the result of one's everyday actions.

As much as we must acknowledge fate, Emerson wrote, even in such dire times we are no less compelled to affirm "liberty, the significance of the individual, the grandeur of duty, the power of character." But, he continued, one must recall that "Nature is no sentimentalist." "The diseases, the elements, fortune, gravity, lightning, respect no persons." Although once the individual thought "positive power was all," now one had to acknowledge "negative power, or circumstance." But the central point remained that, "though Fate is immense, so is Power," for "Power attends and antagonizes Fate." If one capitulates and says "Fate is all," one misses the crucial fact that "part of Fate is the freedom of man."[69] Here as elsewhere in the collection, Emerson replaces spiritual ecstasy with ethical action, the visionary with the moral.[70]

The Civil War

When the Civil War began in 1861, Emerson, like many Americans, was surprised at the South's outright belligerence. That the states in this region might secede had always seemed possible, but outright warfare was another matter. "Nothing that has occurred but has been a surprise," he wrote in his journal. "This revolution," he continued, "is the work of no man" but is "the effervescence of nature." No one individual, "not an abolitionist, not an idealist, can say without effrontery, I did it."[71]

As the battles dragged on with terrible casualties on both sides, Emerson insisted, contra President Lincoln, that the war was not for the preservation of the Union but for emancipation of the slaves. "The war for the Union," he wrote in the war's first year, "is broader than any state policy of sectional interest," for the Union was "not broad enough, because of slavery." "We must come to emancipation," he urged, "with compensation to loyal states" (for "Border" states Delaware, Kentucky, Maryland, and Missouri, which had not seceded), for this was a "principle, [and] everything else," an "intrigue."[72]

After Lincoln issued his preliminary Emancipation Proclamation in the fall of 1862, Emerson delivered a celebratory address in Boston. "Against all timorous counsels," Emerson proclaimed, Lincoln "had the courage to seize the moment."[73] Emerson also penned an occasional poem, "Boston Hymn," for another celebration at the first of the year. During the war, he contributed to various fundraising events, for black orphans and for the all-black Massachusetts Fifty-Fourth Regiment. When its white leader, Boston's Colonel Robert Gould Shaw, and many of his troops were killed, Emerson praised them in a poem, "Voluntaries," published in the *Atlantic Monthly* in October 1863.

Shocked by the regiment's loss and the war's interminable length, Emerson also worried about Britain's lackluster support for the North's position, probably a result of the blockade of Southern ports that greatly reduced supplies of cotton for Britain's immense textile industry. Pressure by Northern "Copperheads," who pushed for a rapid negotiation to end the fighting, also upset him; for Emerson insisted that the North could not now lose faith in what he believed the war's ultimate purpose, the total elimination of slavery. At this unsettled time, evidence of Emerson's awareness of and disappointment in his nation's inability to address their most serious challenges can be seen in "The Fortune of the Republic," an address he presented before the [Theodore] Parker Society in 1863, in the darkest days of the Civil War and repeated at many venues as late as 1878 at Boston's Old South Church.

In this lecture, he excoriated what he regarded as England's rank materialism, which led to that country's moral ambivalence when it came to the North's cause. Because of Lincoln's recent Emancipation Proclamation, however, Emerson recognized that the country was undergoing a "Second Declaration of Independence," which provided the opportunity once again to free themselves from English influence, albeit now in the economic sphere. He urged his countrymen to "cast out the passion for Europe" and work to solidify once and for all their position as the embodiment of "the sentiment and the future of mankind."[74]

But in the sections that he added for the address's later delivery, as Reconstruction was ending, he acknowledged that the United States still had work to do before achieving this position, a disappointment evident as well in poet Walt Whitman's contemporaneous diatribe in his prose *Democratic Vistas* (1871). Where was the self-reliant man in politics, a topic he had broached years before, Emerson asked. The spirit of the country's political economy, he reported, was low and degrading because of materialism's corrosive influence. In the 1870s, Americans saw the great party of property and education, the Republicans, merely "driveling and huckstering away . . . every principle of humanity and the dearest hopes of mankind." The great men of American politics, Emerson continued, "succumb so far to the forms of the day as to peril their integrity for the sake of adding to the weight of their personal character [or] the authority of office." Political parties keep their old names, he noticed, "but exhibit a surprising fugacity in creeping out of one snake-skin into another of equal ignominy and lubricity."[75]

The citizenry seemed no better. The American marches with a careless swagger to the height of power, he observed, heedless of his own liberty or of other peoples', "in his reckless confidence that he can have all that he wants." The American risked "all the prized charters of the human race, bought with battles and revolutions and religion, gambling them all away for a paltry selfish gain."[76] When peoples' voting was rash and irrational, it was not purposeful malignity so much as mere recklessness that bought someone an election.

Now and then, Emerson noted, the result of an election alarmed the people by "the all but unanimous choice of a rogue and brawler." And how did this happen? This was done by the very men you know, he told his auditory, who were "scared or warped into some association in their mind of the candidate with the interest of their trade or their property." In the United States, there was simply "a great sensualism," a headlong devotion to trade and the conquest of the continent—to each man as large a share as he can carve out for himself—and misplaced confidence in our talent and activity, which risks becoming "a scornful materialism" that has no depth.[77]

All was now movement and activity. Emerson had counseled a repose based in acknowledgment of the laws of the universe rather than in the board of trade, but Americans had become slight and vain. The country was now a "wild democracy; the riot of mediocrity and dishonesties and fudges." Young men lacked idealism and only hoped for material gain. The flowering of civilization, Emerson reminded his listeners, was "the finished man, the man of sense, of grace, of accomplishment, of social power," but he had not yet appeared in the United States. The new times need a new man, he said, the "complemental" rather than the commercial man.[78] Spirituality, newly redefined, had to be grounded morally and socially, not in some private, individual quest.

For his part, Emerson continued to believe in the imperial self, but in a new way. One still had to have proper vision, seeing the world as it truly is, as he had counseled as far back as 1836, but that now implied seeing for the purpose of acting ethically: there was a direct link between perception and moral action. He took comfort in what he always had known from the day years earlier when he had stood amazed in the Jardin des Plantes, that the world, as Darwin had shown, was ever changing, always evolving, and always to some good end. The United States itself was part of this eternal process. At every moment, some one country more than any other represents "the sentiment and the future of mankind," he exhorted. The United States, for better or worse, now occupied that place. In the wake of war and reunion, the nation was just settling for itself "questions which, as they shall be determined in one way or another, will make the peace and property or the calamity of the next ages."[79]

Fortunately, the United States was a representative democracy in which citizens could vote for necessary change. As the globe keeps its identity "by perpetual change," he noted, so our civil system, by "perpetual appeal to the people and acceptance of its reforms." The "Genius or Destiny of America" was no sluggard, but incessantly advancing, "as the shadow on the dial's face, or the heavenly body by whose light it is marked." If Americans realized that their country was "the great charity of God to the human race," they would keep it on the right course. Then, Emerson prophesied, trade and government would not be the favored aims of mankind, but "every useful, every elegant art, every exercise of imagination, the height of reason, the noblest affection, the purest religion" would find a home in the nation's institutions.[80] An individual would be valued by what he or she chose to do in an ever-changing world, and one's understanding became the product of one's successive actions.

Afterglow

Despite the darker mood of his later essays, a result both of his personal tragedies and of his disgust at the quickly fraying bonds of citizenship as the nation continued to struggle with its many problems, these later works only solidified Emerson's reputation. After the Civil War, he was celebrated as an American institution, revered in England, France, and other European countries as well as by his fellow citizens.

Adam Mickiewicz, the Polish patriot and poet in exile in Paris, crowed enthusiastically about Emerson's work. It gave him ammunition to argue against Poland's continuing political subjugation, for Emerson's ideas had at their center "the belief in the uninterrupted influence of the invisible world upon the visible."[81] So did Alphonse de Lamartine, a hero of the abortive revolution in France in 1848. Late in life, as he grew ill, he remarked, "The man on earth I so wish to see is Emerson."[82] In an assessment of American literature, the important French critic Philarète Chasles called Emerson "the most original man produced by the United States up to this day."[83]

Emerson was equally praised in England. When Charles Dickens wrote in his *American Notes* (1842) about his recent visit to the United States, he had much to say about Emerson and the movement that he headed. Carlyle agreed. Now a literary lion, he continued his lengthy correspondence with his transatlantic friend and everywhere touted Emerson's work. Matthew Arnold, John Ruskin, and Arthur Hugh Clough were admirers. Following Emerson's trip to England in 1846 to 1847, one English journal spoke of an "Emerson mania" that had overcome the country.[84]

However, Emerson's most enthusiastic reception remained in the United States. Those who found his philosophy obscure parodied or mocked his words, but he was still a household name, the country's representative man of letters. His philosophy affected not only those who circled his sphere but also people farther afield: women's rights advocates and social reformers of all stripes, educators, and not insignificantly, businessmen.

In 1844, for example, Emerson had met and befriended Frederick Douglass, a relationship that only grew stronger as war loomed. They shared the dais at the invitation of the Concord Female Anti-Slavery Society, when Emerson spoke movingly in celebration of England's emancipation of slaves in the British West Indies. In the early years of Reconstruction, Douglass's most frequent speech was the Emerson-inflected "Self-Made Men."[85] A committee of New York's black abolitionists responded to Gerrit Smith's offer of land for resettlement in upstate New York by noting that they must "assiduously" practice "self-reliance," and an African American poet penned a poetic tribute to Emerson's popular essay.[86] Emerson knew abolitionist John Brown, too, welcoming him into his home when Brown visited Concord, and endorsed his intention to raise money for arms to take to "Bleeding Kansas." He gave memorial remarks in both Boston and nearby Salem after Brown's hanging.

In her epochal *Woman in the Nineteenth Century*, Margaret Fuller had adapted and applied Emerson's self-reliance to women's position. "We would have every arbitrary barrier thrown down," she proclaimed. "We would have every path laid open to Woman as freely as to Man." "Let us be wise, and not impede the soul," she continued. "Let us have one creative energy, one incessant revelation."[87]

Emerson greatly admired Fuller. He even chose her to coedit the transcendentalist periodical *The Dial*. After Fuller's premature death at sea during a hurricane while returning from Europe, Emerson sent Thoreau to Fire Island, New York, to look for her remains or any of her manuscripts that might have survived; he returned only with a button from her young son's coat. In 1852, with the help of two of her friends, James Freeman Clarke and William Henry Channing, Emerson edited her *Memoirs*. She had led him to consider the cause of women more widely. In the 1850s he began to speak regularly at women's rights conventions. By the 1870s, women's advocate Susan B. Anthony regularly cited him in support of her cause in her *Woman's Journal*. Emerson was following his own counsel to act in the world, every day, for one's fellow citizens and so display how what was moral did indeed shine through what one accomplished, not through mere contemplation.

In his influential "The Gospel of Wealth" (1880), steel magnate Andrew Carnegie retooled Emersonian individualism for use in strictly secular terms. "You cannot push any one up a ladder," he noted, "unless he be willing to climb a little himself." "Aim for the highest," he urged (Emerson had crowed, "Hitch your wagon to a star"). "Think of yourself as on the threshold of unparalleled success. A whole, clear, glorious life lies before you. Achieve! Achieve!"[88] Budding environmentalists, too, embraced the man now known as the "Concord Sage." In the 1870s on one of his cross-country lecture tours, Emerson met an enthusiastic admirer, the future advocate for national parks, John Muir, near Yosemite. They became correspondents, Muir later remembering Emerson as "the most serene, sequoia-like soul I ever met."[89] On the other side of the country, in upstate New York, nature writer John Burroughs recalled first reading Emerson in 1856, after which Emerson's philosophy greatly influenced him. Later, Burroughs wrote elegantly about him and his close friend and fellow transcendentalist Thoreau.

The French diplomat and political scientist Alexis de Tocqueville had used a newly minted word, "individualism," to describe what after his visit to the United States in the 1830s he believed explained much about the country. He distinguished it from "selfishness." The former was "a reflective and peaceable sentiment," he explained, that disposes each citizen to isolate one's self from the mass of those like one and to withdraw to one side with family and friends, so that after having thus created a little society for one's own use, one willingly "abandons society at large to itself." Selfishness, he explained, is a passionate and exaggerated love of self that makes one relate everything to the self alone and to prefer it to everything else.

However, Tocqueville condemned both, for if selfishness was born of blind instinct, individualism proceeded from erroneous judgment, its source in defects of the mind as much as vices of the heart. While selfishness "withers the seed of all the virtues," individualism dries up the source of public virtues, and in the long run, "attacks and destroys all the others and will finally be absorbed in selfishness."[90]

Tocqueville could have been describing the fate of Emerson's thought in the post–Civil War period when aggrandization of self often worked to the detriment of society. Jonathan Edwards had offered a view of heaven on earth that was completely God centered. Emerson installed and retrained the individual at the world's center, first as a connoisseur of spiritual ecstasy, later as a champion of moral character that reflected universal order. After the Civil War his views, often misunderstood, became a part of the nation's self-understanding, a cornerstone of national mythology.[91]

The Gilded Age, though, with its enormous inequalities of wealth and deteriorating social conditions, demanded a new philosopher, someone who would further right the balance between God and self, self and society, and liberty and justice. In his later works, Emerson had begun to show the way toward the kind of ethical pragmatism that was needed, for he understood that all one can ever have are provisional truths that soon enough are replaced by others, equally provisional. In such a world, freedom consists of an understanding that moral choices are ever before one and that, in the face of them, one has to display character and act ethically. Serendipitously, someone whose family was intimately connected to Emerson himself soon enough took up where he left off.

3
William James
THE ACTIVE LIFE

What to Do?

In the late winter of 1842, Ralph Waldo Emerson made his first lecture appearance in New York City at the New York Society Library, one of whose members was Henry James Sr.[1] The lecture so impressed James that immediately on returning home he wrote Emerson a letter in which he lavishly praised his performance and invited him to visit. Eager to meet him, he took the liberty of calling on Emerson at his hotel, where they had a several-hours conversation. Thus, began a lifelong friendship, for James believed that he had finally found the intellectual and spiritual soulmate he had been seeking. For his part, Emerson enjoyed the lively conversation of his new friend. Writing to his wife, he noted that, of all the people he had met in New York, Henry James was "the best apple on the tree." One of Emerson's Boston friends, the poet James Russell Lowell, agreed. He thought James "the best talker in America."[2]

During this same trip to New York, Emerson visited the James family at their home at Five Washington Place. Family legend has it that the couple took him upstairs to see their first child, two-month-old William.[3] Through Williams's formative years, Emerson was so frequent a visitor to the James home that the family referred to the spare bedroom as "Mr. Emerson's room." "I often found myself thinking," Henry James once confessed, "if this man were a woman, I should be sure to fall in love with him."[4]

Emerson's transcendentalism fascinated James, but at first, he had trouble comprehending it. "Oh you man without a handle!" he exclaimed in exasperation after being dissatisfied with one of Emerson's letters.[5] Nor was James reticent to offer his new friend more pointed advice. Emerson's great flaw, James once wrote him, was his outright rejection of Calvinism. What the country needed, he continued, was "Jonathan Edwards *redivivus* in true blue." That person "would, after an honest study of the philosophy that has grown up since his day, make the best possible reconciler and critic of philosophy."[6] Over a fifty-year career as a writer, lecturer, and public intellectual, James himself, as much as he admired Edwards, tried but could not fill that role. However, his son William did.

William had difficulty finding a vocation. At first, he thought of attending Union College, but his father had no fond recollections of his own time there—he had been rather profligate, running up huge bills for alcohol, cigars, and foppish clothes, to *his* father's chagrin—and discouraged him. In fact, because their father had a low opinion of almost *any* formal schooling, the Jameses educated their five children (in addition to William and Henry they were Alice, Garth Wilkinson, and Robertson) primarily by private tutors, either at home or on the family's frequent trips to Europe.

At the age of eighteen, William was thin, just over five feet eight inches tall, and weighed about 130 pounds. His dark hair covered part of his ears, and he sported a thin, boyish mustache. He had dark brown and piercing eyes that spoke to the scarcely submerged energy of his entire personality. His father had set his heart on a career in science for his oldest child, but William, having shown a talent for drawing (and a recurrent rebellious streak against his overbearing parent), wanted instead to become an artist. His father reluctantly indulged his son's interest. The teenager showed so much promise that, when the James family lived in Newport, Rhode Island, between 1860 and 1861, acclaimed painter William Morris Hunt accepted him for lessons in his studio.

However, in 1861, still unsure of what he wanted to do, he abruptly abandoned the easel. His sister, Alice, neatly captured her brother's frequent tendency to vacillate. He was "just like a blob of mercury," she wrote; "you can't put a mental finger on him."[7] Next, with the

Civil War breaking out, like so many other young men he wondered whether he should enlist in the Union army. He signed on to the Newport Artillery Company, a state militia, for a three-month stint, making bandages and rolling bullets. He very much wanted to join the action, but his father did not want any of his sons to serve. To a friend he wrote that he "had a firm grasp for three days upon the coat-tails of my Willy and Harry, who both vituperate me beyond measure because I won't let them go off."[8] Two years later the elder James was not able to stop younger son Garth Wilkinson (known as Wilky) from enlisting. Wilky joined Colonel Robert Gould Shaw's ill-fated Fifty-Fourth Massachusetts Regiment and in the disastrous attack on Fort Wagner, South Carolina, was severely wounded.

Still unsure of his career, William pleased his father by enrolling at the Lawrence Scientific School, founded at Harvard in 1847 and overseen by the recent Swiss émigré Louis Agassiz, a highly respected naturalist. At the new school, rather than taking a series of classes, students worked closely with a single professor. James chose to study chemistry with Charles William Eliot, a mediocre scientist who would later become famous as Harvard's most transformative president.

The Lawrence School was riding a wave of interest in science, particularly in geology, chemistry, and natural history. Charles Darwin had just published his *On the Origin of Species*, setting off spirited debates about the truth of his theories.[9] James found himself in the thick of the fight, for Agassiz was among Darwin's chief American detractors, while the well-regarded professor of botany Asa Gray ardently supported evolutionary theory. James read Darwin's *Origin* as early as September 1863, and it left an indelible mark.[10] From the highly mechanized Northern factories churning out war materiel, including the weapons that caused such carnage at Gettysburg and Bull Run, to the latest scientific scholarship that impacted social theory—the prime example, Herbert Spencer and William Graham Sumner's advocacy of social Darwinism, which popularized the phrase "survival of the fittest"—powerful winds of change were transforming citizen and nation.

William enjoyed Cambridge both intellectually and socially. The best Boston families knew the Jameses, guaranteeing a constant flow of invitations to dinners and dances. The most important friendship he formed was with Charles Sanders Peirce, son of the college's professor of mathematics and, later, a brilliant philosopher. In such company James flourished, staying on for two years and then devoting another semester to his own reading. Though he now intended to make a career in medicine, he read widely in literature and philosophy as well. One book on his list was Jonathan Edwards's *Great Christian Doctrine of Original Sin Defended*, from which James took copious notes. He did not agree fully with the theologian's arguments but, like his father, acknowledged that evil was something real in the world that men and women had to confront.

In 1863, while Wilky was home suffering from the terrible wounds from which he would never fully recover, James returned to Cambridge to study physiology and comparative anatomy. He worked his way through Darwin's book, approvingly. By the end of the year, he had changed direction again and decided to attend the Harvard Medical School, another recent addition to the university's courses of study.

A year later, after James had completed most of his work at the medical school, Agassiz offered him the opportunity to accompany him on an expedition to the upper reaches of the Amazon River. Intent on debunking Darwin's theories, Agassiz wanted to collect different species of fish and other fauna across the immense Amazon basin to prove that each was a unique creation of God. Over the course of five months, traveling by steamship and then by small boat or canoe, William James, twenty-three, covered five thousand miles. He won Agassiz's confidence and was frequently put in charge of the many trips up tributaries that Agassiz ordered to secure more specimens. Even as he began to doubt the validity of Agassiz's beliefs concerning evolution, the basin's flora, fauna, and human inhabitants thrilled him. Agassiz in turn appreciated James's artistic talent and scientific acumen. The naturalist's book-length account of the expedition, *A Journey in Brazil* (1869), included engravings from his pupil's sketches.

But James, who was seriously ill part of the time, eventually realized that he did not want to continue such fieldwork, for he enjoyed speculation more than collection, preservation, and classification. He returned to Cambridge and finished his course at the medical school, where he now made another lifelong friend, Oliver Wendell Holmes Jr., who had seen much action in the Civil War and now had matriculated at Harvard's law school. After completing his course work in medicine, James served for a few months as a general surgeon at the Massachusetts General Hospital, but things still did not feel right. He was overworked and ill, and then he threw out his back during a dissecting session and for weeks could hardly walk. Falling into one of his frequent depressions, he decided to abandon the practice of medicine.

Following his family's habit, he sailed to Europe to recuperate. He stopped first in Paris and then, for a longer time, in Dresden, where he read widely in German, including Goethe and Hegel, and finally made his way to a water spa in Bohemia, where the baths unfortunately failed to improve his health. In September 1867, in a letter to his father marked "Private," he opened his darkened soul to the man under whose influence and with whose ideas he had grappled for years. James was troubled, even suicidal. "Thoughts of pistol, the dagger and the bowl begin to usurp an unduly large part of my attention," he admitted.[11]

Paternal Bonds

Henry James Sr. had been raised in Albany in the strict Presbyterian faith and in 1835 had enrolled in the Princeton Theological Seminary, a conservative bastion then overseen by the redoubtable systematic theologian Charles Hodge.[12] The religious temperature at Princeton was high because its professors, mostly Presbyterians, were fighting battles on two fronts—against New England's liberal Unitarians as well as those in their own denomination who embraced the "New Measures" of upstate–New York evangelist Charles Grandison Finney, who devoted himself to revivalist preaching. Attending classes in the middle of these battles, the elder James commenced a circuitous religious pilgrimage that finally found him a devoted follower of the eighteenth-century Swedish mystic Emanuel Swedenborg.[13]

Swedenborg placed God at the center of the universe, but his was a very different deity from that which Presbyterians worshipped. Contra the latter group's belief in mankind's innate depravity, Swedenborg stressed God's essential goodness to humankind, believing that the divine afflatus flowed through all people.[14] This argued their irreducible equality. Further, Swedenborg believed that nature corresponded directly to the world of spirit and thus offered a language that enabled mankind to discern one's true relation to God. To Swedenborg, the spiritual world was reality, the visible universe but a mirror of the divine greatness. When Emerson had encountered this correspondential theory in 1826 in American Swedenborgian Sampson Reed's *Observations on the Growth of the Mind*, it awakened his own interest in the religion. Now, the erstwhile Presbyterian James was similarly enthralled.

In the 1840s, however, the elder James also attended nondenominational church meetings at Stuyvesant Hall in New York City, where Christian socialist William Henry Channing, nephew of the great Unitarian leader William Ellery Channing, preached. Channing awakened in James a lifelong interest in social reform and the new study of "social science." Under Channing's influence, the elder James began to drift away from Emersonian transcendentalism as well as criticize contemporary Swedenborgians' emphasis on organized churches and the ritual they practiced.

James's chief point of contention with Emerson was the high value the latter placed on self-reliance. "The grand disturbing element in human affairs," James wrote, "the one great obstacle to the Providential evolution of human destiny," was nothing less than "the spirit of individualism, the spirit which prompts man to aggrandize himself at the expense of the common wealth." He longed for the day when, just as "the individual had risen to the brother," then "the brother to the neighbor," and then "the neighbor to the citizen," so eventually the citizen would "rise into the MAN,—rise into unity with all his race, giving to all men an equal regard, because all men have the same divine parentage, and the same divine destiny."[15]

Toward this end, one had to strive to extinguish or, as James put it memorably (quoting Swedenborg), "defecate" the self. "Self-sufficiency," he wrote, is "the only evil known to the spiritual universe," for it leads to the "renunciation of God from the life" and prevents one from experiencing divine love.[16] James's contemporaries should not cultivate strict self-reliance, as Emerson urged, but strive to live a life of Christian humility and charity. Separation from other human beings was hell. If one subdued the self, union with others would bring one closer to God. Salvation depended on opening oneself to an influx of divine love that made possible a union with all humankind who share in it. The title of one of James's many books, *Society the Redeemed Form of Man* (1879), perfectly captures his belief.

That autumn William was struggling with his father's complex religious ideas when he exchanged several more letters with him, trying to understand his parent's confidence in a beneficent universe even as his own depression deepened. James doubted many things about his father's voluminous theological writings, objecting to his prolix prose but more to the "darkness which to me has always hung over what you have written." Then he got more personal. "You live in such mental isolation," William wrote, "that I cannot help often feeling bitterly at the thought that you must see in even your own children strangers to what you consider the best part of yourself."[17]

James could never accept his parent's assured and unbending monism, a view of the universe in which God was the only being. Given his training in natural science, William was ready to substitute the material for the spiritual, much as European positivists like Auguste Comte did. There was only the individual, the self, in the here and now, he thought. Beginning to formulate beliefs that were diametrically opposed to his father's, he declared, "We ourselves must be our own providence."[18]

James was living a in a world that the Civil War had irrevocably transformed. Thousands of miles of rails now linked hitherto disparate parts of the nation, shrinking notions of physical distance. Steamboats plied the country's great rivers and likewise contributed to the nation's various regions' growing sense that they were part of an intricately linked union. Even temporality assumed new meaning, with the rapid transfer of information via the telegraph giving a new sense to "the news." At an unprecedented rate, immense steam-powered factories turned out household goods as well as iron and steel building materials, forever eclipsing the ubiquitous trade workshops. Within a few years, electricity would light public buildings, typesetting machines would simplify and accelerate the printing of newspapers and books, and typewriters would transform the very act of writing.

Belief in science and progress was replacing an older worldview centered either on the divine or on an all-sufficient imperial self. This led to challenges that the elder James could never fully meet but that his son tackled head-on and assimilated into an ethic fit for modernity. Foremost, he had to reconcile how the autonomous individual fit into a social order over which one seemed to have decreasing control. James's answer was to stress the power of volition. To him, free will was not a platitude but that which one constantly had to assert against the world, much as Emerson had struggled to reconcile "power" and "fate."

Loss and Redemption

As he pondered these questions, James next went to Berlin, where he remained for a year and a half, taking advanced courses in physiology at the university. It became clear that he did not so much want to study the medical healing arts as the physical foundations and formations of consciousness. One of the intellectual oases of Europe, Berlin was a center for such work. He announced to his father that "as a central point of study I imagine that the border ground of physiology and psychology, overlapping both, would be as fruitful as any." He had finally begun to imagine a career.[19]

In March 1869, Harvard chose James's chemistry instructor Eliot as its president, who soon began an overhaul of the school and its curriculum that inaugurated a new era in American higher education. In response to the exodus of young Americans flocking to France and Germany for serious graduate training (particularly in the sciences and modern languages) that hardly existed in the United States, Eliot began—professor by professor, course by course, building by building, school by school—to restructure the university on the European model. He sought to modernize Harvard and to offer a new kind of education, one that better prepared students for the demands and opportunities of the new age.

James returned to Cambridge in the spring of 1869, completed his thesis and examination requirements, and received an MD, the only degree Harvard ever awarded him. However, he was still not quite his own man. He continued to vacillate about his vocation and to spar with his demanding parent. That autumn his father's book *The Secret of Swedenborg* appeared. It was a difficult read, received critical reviews, and never found an audience. When novelist William Dean Howells (who had been raised a Swedenborgian) reviewed it for the *Atlantic Monthly*, he quipped, "Mr. Henry James has written a book called *The Secret of Swedenborg* and has kept it." James's new friend Peirce also reviewed it. He criticized the author's "ignorance of the way of thinking of other men, and his cool neglect of their difficulties." For his part, James said that, even though his father's latest work contained some "great and original ideas," there were "many points which before were incomprehensible to me because doubtfully fallacious" but which he now knew "to be entirely fallacious."[20]

Through these months, James fell into another depression that only deepened after the death of his young, vivacious, and much adored cousin Minnie Temple. With dark hair, large eyes, and a direct, unsettling gaze, she was his favorite, full of restless energy and an esprit that made her delightful company. She was, William later said, "unique and without analogue in all my subsequent experience of people."[21] She loved to read, especially George Eliot's novels, and could not wait to hear what her friends said about Robert Browning's new work, *The*

Ring and the Book. And she delighted in William as much as he did in her. Rumor had it that Minnie and he might in fact be in love, even though they both knew any deeper tie was unlikely, because of their consanguinity and her increasing severe illness. William's brother Henry also adored Minnie and modeled Isabel Archer, the unforgettable heroine of *The Portrait of a Lady*, on her.

In the late autumn of 1869, as Minnie wasted away from tuberculosis, James was shattered. The depth of his despair is evident in his diary. "Today," he wrote, "I about touched bottom, and perceive plainly that I must face the choice with open eyes: shall I frankly throw the moral business overboard . . . or shall I follow it, and it alone, making everything else mere stuff of it?"[22] By "moral business," he meant the belief that man, endowed with free will, was not powerless in a universe that seemed predetermined, that could, for example, permit tragedy like Minnie's disease.

After her death, James addressed her in his diary. "Minnie, your death makes me feel the nothingness of our egotistical fury." What we must learn to do, he continued, is, "ascend to some sort of partnership with fate, and since tragedy is at the heart of us, go to meet it, work it to our ends, instead of dodging it all our days, and being run down by it at last."[23] James took these words to heart and placed them at the center of much of his subsequent work.

Minnie Temple's death brought William James to a dark place similar to where Emerson had found himself after the death of his five-year-old son, Waldo. Fate had chastened both men, crushing them by a turn of events that they could neither effect nor fully understand. Emerson came through the other side of his tragedy and in his essay "Experience" reported what it had done to him. He marched on, a changed but undefeated man. Now James, too, had to take stock, marshal his powers, and find a way forward.

It was not easy. One evening in early 1870, he went into a dressing room to procure something, when, as he later explained, "suddenly there fell upon me without any warning, just as if it came out of the darkness, a horrible fear of my own existence." All he could think of was of an epileptic he had recently seen in an asylum, "a black-haired youth with greenish skin," someone "entirely idiotic, who used to sit all day on one of the benches . . . with his knees drawn up to his chin." He looked, James continued, "like a sort of sculptured Egyptian cat or Peruvian mummy, moving nothing but his black eyes and looking absolutely non-human." There was "such a perception of my own merely momentary discrepancy from him, that it was as if something hitherto solid within my breast gave way entirely, and I became a mass of quivering fear." This fear was so invasive and powerful, James recalled, "that if I had not clung to scripture texts like 'the eternal God is my refuge,' etc., 'Come unto me, all ye that labor and are heavy-laden,' etc., 'I am the resurrection and the life,' etc. I think I should have grown really insane."[24]

It was a signal experience. James's recent reengagement with his father's works, Minnie's heartfelt and stoic letters to him describing her religious state and impending death, and what James later understood as his "acute neurasthenic attack with phobia," all brought him face to face with the question of religious belief.[25] He sought solace in reading. While abroad, he had encountered the work of philosopher Charles Renouvier (1815–1903), once an advocate of French socialist Charles Fourier's utopianism but now combating the philosophical movement called positivism, led by Auguste Comte. Positivists believed that they could measure and assess anything worth knowing; they were "scientists" through and through. They prided themselves on uncovering the primal physical laws that determined everything, from matter to the shape of human society. One corollary of such thought was that, just as all things obeyed immutable laws, so too did human life. This essentially obviated any hint of man or woman's free will. Humanity was powerless against the universe's great natural laws, such as gravity or evolution through natural selection.

James would have none of it. During this dark time, he lit on the notion of heroic resistance to fate. What mattered most in the moral life was how one responded to circumstance. The good soul is the active one. However, how would James himself answer this challenge?

How would he stand against the vagaries of fate and the weight of a universe that chance seemed to rule? The answer lay in the intersection of physiology, psychology, and philosophy. For the next year, he read voraciously in all three fields. He also attended meetings of the Metaphysical Club, organized in Cambridge in 1871 by mathematician and philosopher Chauncey Wright, whose members—including Oliver Wendell Holmes Jr., Charles Sanders Peirce, and several other of Cambridge's intellectuals—ushered in a golden era of philosophical thought in American culture.[26] Then, in 1873, Eliot, as part of his masterplan to rebuild Harvard, hired James to teach physiology, "the science of life." Parting his hair in the middle, with a full beard and mustache, still slender, and dressing in clothes that were often of an "entrancing, unfamiliar cut" that caught everyone's attention, James entered the classroom. He was a born teacher.

Thinking and Acting

In 1870, as part of his attempt to improve graduate-level instruction at Harvard, Eliot invited Emerson to participate in a new series of university lectures delivered by prominent intellectuals who were not members of the university faculty. Other participants included philosopher and historian John Fiske, transcendentalist minister Frederic Henry Hedge, and philosopher and mathematician Peirce, among others. It was the first time that the university had reached out to Emerson since 1838, when he had outraged the divinity school with his daring address to the graduating class. Emerson generously obliged, offering lectures on the "Natural History of the Intellect," which he had outlined in the late 1840s and now reworked.

Against the empirical and positivist strains in contemporary philosophy, Emerson defended the idealism that he had first enunciated in 1836. To him, nature was the symbol of spirit. But given advances in physiology and psychology, he now argued that one should carefully enumerate the laws and powers of the mind. He, like James, was beginning to understand that one had to apply the rigor of scientific method to the study of consciousness. Although Emerson only sketched the outlines of such a project, others in Cambridge's intellectual elite—most notably members of the Metaphysical Club—also believed that this exploration of consciousness was central to an understanding of how the mind worked and might provide the basis for a new moral order. They were eager to hear what the sage of Concord would add to their ruminations.

Intellect, Emerson proclaimed in his first lecture, builds the universe and is the key to all it contains, for in all sciences the student discovers "that nature is always working, in whole and in every detail, after the laws of the human mind."[27] But one should not stop with mere metaphysical speculation. Beliefs had to be perpetually reinforced by life, by what one did in response to the cards one was dealt. A reply to fate, whether that involved challenges from one's environment, overreaching by the state, or the limitations of one's own inherited predispositions, *was* biography.

Emerson reminded his audience that, by extension, "the mind is the creator of the world, and is ever creating," for matter is nothing but "dead Mind" until the individual consciousness makes sense of it.[28] This Emerson, of "Self-Reliance" and *The American Scholar*, who trumpeted individualism in both the search for spiritual knowledge and one's engagement in social reform, had been important to James as he searched for a vocation. Now, however, he understood Emerson's advice in new ways. Emerson's creed, he wrote at the age of forty, was simply "that everything that ever was or will be is here in the enveloping now; that man has but to obey himself." This thought, James continued, "exorcis[ed] . . . all scepticism" as to the power of one's natural faculties.[29]

James found himself drifting more and more toward psychology and philosophy. He angled with President Eliot for a position in the Philosophy Department as soon as its senior professor, Francis Bowen, retired. James also developed a substantial résumé. In 1877 he published his first essay, in the *Journal of Speculative Philosophy*, a

St. Louis–based journal edited by the American Hegelian William T. Harris, in which James picked a fight with the highly regarded English philosopher Herbert Spencer. By focusing exclusively on the process of cognition, James wrote, Spencer simply ignored a whole range of reactions that are centered in the mind. Aesthetic impulses, sentiments, religious emotions, and personal affections: all these have a role in consciousness. Not a thought occurs, James argued, "but feeling is there to comment on it, stamp it of greater or less worth."[30]

James understood the mind, or what is more properly called consciousness, as "intelligent intelligence," supplying, as he put it, "the means and a standard by which [things] are measured." In his memorable formulation, "the knower is not simply a mirror floating with no foothold anywhere, and passively reflecting an order that he comes upon and finds simply existing." He is himself "an actor, and coefficient of truth on one side, whilst on the other he registers the truth which he helps create."[31]

James also continued his public lectures and presented six on "The Brain and the Mind" in the fall of 1878 at Boston's renowned Lowell Institute. Here he moved effortlessly between physiology and psychology. It was time, he urged, to recognize the importance of the "subjective method" to understand the mind. Rejecting both positivism and abstruse metaphysics, he argued for the ever-active mind. "Every act," he said, "leaves a trace in the individual," becomes a part of who one is and what one does. "The great thing," he continued, is to form habits that then allow one "to imagine and realize new things," the more those habits are "unbroken and constant."[32]

As he thought through these matters, James returned to questions he had asked when he first had read Darwin. Why, he wondered, was consciousness so important in evolution? What did it give humanity to set it apart from other animals? "If consciousness can load the dice," James wrote, if it can exert a constant pressure in the right direction through habit; if the individual "can feel what nerve processes are leading to the goal, can reinforce and strengthen these and at the same time inhibit those which threaten to lead us astray," consciousness will have proved of invaluable service in humankind's survival and evolution.[33] And one loaded the dice by forming habitual responses, reacting the same way to a stimulus the second, third, and fourth time as one had the first. Thus habit, that part of consciousness nurtured over time, helped one survive. This made perfect sense in Darwin's world, even as it gave one power through the ability both to think and act.

Consciousness always compares and selects. When it finally appeared in the evolutionary chain, it marked the end of the reign of chance and inaugurated one of intelligent choice. "I for one," James remarked, "as a scientific and a practical man alike, deny utterly that Science compels me to believe that my conscience is an *ignis fatuus* [will of the wisp] or outcast." He urged his audience to leave his lectures strengthened in the faith that "your delights and sorrows, your loves and hates, your aspirations and efforts are real combatants in life's arena, and not impotent, paralytic spectators of the game."[34] Each person is an active player and develops habits that enable him or her to respond responsibly to its challenges. Not to acknowledge this diminished one's humanity.

James thus continued to praise the centrality of the self even when the nation's rapid industrialization and its attendant dehumanization of the worker made more and more individuals doubt their own agency. Against such behemoths as John D. Rockefeller's Standard Oil or Andrew Carnegie's empire of iron and steel, of what value was a single individual? At this point, should the state step in with regulation to preserve the integrity and ensure the livelihood of each individual; or should it champion what was good for the greatest number?

The Active Life

Philosophy needed to participate in such debates, James believed. If philosophy only "baffles and disappoints our dearest desires and most cherished powers," he wrote, it has to be dismissed as glorified navel-gazing, for "cognition is incomplete until discharged in act." If one surveys history and asks what features all great periods of revival, of expansion of the human mind, displayed in common, James argued, one found "that each and all of them have said to the human being, 'the inmost nature of the reality is congenial to powers which you possess.'"[35] Celebrating such individual empowerment, James argued that if democracy was to succeed as a political ideology, it had to make people believe that they were more than cogs in a Gilded Age machine.

James also directly addressed the subject of faith, a subject of perennial interest to him. For centuries, philosophers had tried to ignore religion, seeking to "huddle" it out of sight "in their pretentions to found systems of absolute certainty." But James redefined religion as "belief in something concerning which doubt is still theoretically possible." Influenced by but unable to put to bed his father's unwavering monistic belief in an Absolute, he observed that we cannot live or think without some degree of faith, for at least it provides a "working hypothesis" about the nature and destiny of man. Faith is necessary as one of "the indispensable conditions for the realization of its objects," he argued. Individuals thus have the opportunity to shape their destiny, for whenever they espouse a cause, they contribute to its determination. Success depends on "energy of act, energy again depends on faith that [they] shall not fail, and that faith in turn in the faith that [they] are right." One has to risk, believing in oneself. "All that the human heart wants," James wrote, "is its chance," and if having faith helps to provide that, it is valuable.[36]

The essay in which James explored this topic appeared in 1882, a difficult year for the James family. Early in January William's mother, Mary, died at the age of seventy-one. The family thought that she was recovering from bronchial asthma, but by late January she took a turn for the worse and died. To her son Henry she was "the sweetest, gentlest, most natural embodiment of maternity—and our protecting spirit, our household genius."[37] Her life had not been easy. She had been in charge of a household with five children, her sister Catharine, and five Irish servant girls as well as her admittedly chauvinistic husband, who was utterly dependent on her. Henry was her favorite son, but she was closest to her semi-invalid daughter, Alice. Mary always found William difficult, partly for his periodic illnesses as well as for his seeming lack of direction, but he recognized that she held the household together. By this time some of the other children were scattered—Henry was in Washington, D.C., William was in Chicago, and Wilky in Milwaukee—but all were able to join Alice and another brother, ne'er-do-well Bob, for her funeral.

Then in April Emerson died. Both William and Henry attended the funeral, held in Concord's First Church, with interment in nearby Sleepy Hollow Cemetery. The brothers had traveled from Cambridge in a special train, whose other passengers included Eliot, Harvard's president; the poet Oliver Wendell Holmes; author and social critic Charles Eliot Norton; and other luminaries, while hundreds of other people came to Concord in carriages and wagons, or even on foot. The townspeople, ever proud of their most famous resident, adorned every doorway along the funeral route with black-and-white rosettes. Henry called the funeral "a popular manifestation, the most striking I have ever seen provoked by the death of a man of letters."[38]

Then, the following November, there was one more almost unthinkable loss: the family patriarch died. Henry James Sr. recently had had more frequent bouts of nausea and faintness, which one doctor attributed to indigestion. Soon, though, he stopped eating entirely and told Mary's sister Catharine that he had already begun his immortal life. In a letter that Henry read at their father's graveside, William (who was absent in Europe) pondered his father's faith and belief in the afterlife. Ever the empiricist, William had not yet found assurance of life after death. "As for the other side, and Mother, and all our possible meeting, I can't say anything," he wrote, although if an afterlife is real, he added, "all would be solved and justified."[39] "As life closes," he later wrote Henry, "all a man has done seems like one cry or sentence." "Father's cry," he continued, had been "the single one that religion is real."[40] Two decades later James would honor that "cry" in his magisterial *Varieties of Religious Experience.*

Before his father's death, William had been traveling in Europe, where he met several other thinkers who expanded his understanding of consciousness and the self. In Prague psychologist Carl Stumpf squired him around, conversing all the while on his favorite topics, the perception of space and the psychology of music. William also met for several hours with Ernst Mach, a physicist, physiologist, psychologist, and philosopher who was hard at work on his *Science of Mechanics*, which was followed by the even more influential *Principles of the Theory of Heat*. A devoted positivist, Mach believed that nothing should be admissible in science unless it could be empirically verified. Anything that could not be so tested was merely metaphysical and of no interest to him. Mach assumed that Plato and Kant were simply wrong to assume that there was a hidden reality beyond sensation, a possibility that James would keep alive. From Prague James traveled to Berlin, Cologne, and Liège, where he heard psychologist and philosopher Joseph-Rémi-Léopold Delboeuf lecture. Delboeuf was interested in hypnotism, another topic that later engaged James, who avidly pursued the study of spiritualism in spite of positivists' derision at what they regarded as hokum.

Early the following year, in London working on his *Principles of Psychology*, James had a philosophical epiphany. Giving a talk to the "Scratch Eight" group of which he was a member—among the others were Leslie Stephen, editor of *Cornhill Magazine* and father of young Virginia (later to marry Leonard Woolf), and George Croom Robertson, editor of the highly respected journal *Mind*—James lit upon a novel way to describe how humans think: he described "the wonderful stream of our consciousness."

The mental life, he wrote, is "like the bird's life," made of "an alternation of flights and perchings." The trouble with most descriptions of consciousness to date was their overlooking "the transitive parts," the flights of the bird from one perch to another. Men's thoughts are much more than the resting places, he explained. If one viewed the birds' flights only as ways to a conclusion, stopping them to look at them before the conclusion is reached is really annihilating them.

Instead, one must recognize that their movement is "central to what happens next."[41] "Once admit that the passing and evanescent are as real parts of the stream," he continued; "once allow that fringes and haloes, inarticulate perceptions, whereof the objects are as yet unnamed, mere nascencies of cognition, premonition, awareness of direction are thoughts *sui generis*, as much as articulate imaginings and propositions are," one begins to comprehend the complexity of consciousness.[42]

Emerson himself had had a premonition of this idea. In one of his recent lectures on "Intellect" at Harvard he had observed that, "in my thought I seem to stand on the bank of a river and watch the endless flow of the stream, floating objects of all shapes, colors, and natures." Nor could he "detain them as they pass, except by running beside them a little way along the bank." But "whence they come and whither they go is not told to me."[43] This understanding of thought as *motion* undergirded James's *Principles of Psychology*. It also would have an immeasurable effect on art and literature, not the least the novels of his remarkable younger brother Henry and his former Harvard student Gertrude Stein.

A Question of Consent

James labored for years on his immense (2,970 manuscript pages) *Principles of Psychology*. Henry Holt, who had commissioned the work over a decade earlier, accepted the manuscript as it was and published it in the fall of 1890. Within fifteen months, the book had entered its third printing, with almost two thousand copies sold. The public finally had before it a striking synthesis of important new ideas about the self, told in vibrant, memorable prose. In this and his future work, William sought to articulate the proper balance between individual and state, self and community, faith and God. He offered an early modern vision of a robust democracy and spirituality anchored by active, choice-making individuals. If Edwards gave critical agency to God, and Emerson to unerring inner instincts, James placed it in the self-conscious, risk-taking individual, the courageous moral hero who in an often unfriendly universe was not averse to walking on the perilous edge of existence, the better to fulfill has role as democratic citizen.

The Principles of Psychology offered new ways to think about this novel understanding of the self. Consider, for example, James's description of the dark twists of fate, those personal disasters that everyone sometimes experiences. "When a dreadful object is presented, or when life as a whole turns up its dark abysses to our view," and admits of no reply but "the dumb turning of the will and the tightening of our heart-strings as we say, 'Yes, I will even have it so!'" then are we fully alive. When one confronts the world's travails—even horrors—rather than evidencing an "ostrich-like forgetfulness," the individual must find "zest" in the challenge.[44]

When one meets difficulty head-on, James argued, one becomes "one of the masters and the lords of life" (a reference to Emerson's great essay "Experience"). When one takes risks, one participates in and helps shape human destiny. Neither in theory nor in practice, he reminded readers, "do we care for, or go for help to, those who have no heads for risks, or sense for living on the perilous edge." We should not place any faith or confidence in such moral cowards. "'Will you or won't you have it so?'" James declared, is the most "probing" question we are ever asked. Whether or not we realize it, we confront such questions every hour of every day, about the largest as well as the smallest, the most theoretical and the most practical, matters. "We answer," he concluded, "by consents or non-consents, not by words," a sentiment strikingly akin to Edwards's notion that "the will is as the greatest apparent good is," that is, that the matter of choice or consent is central to our humanity.[45]

Despite the success of James's *Psychology* and his satisfaction with teaching, he soon confronted more personal sadness. In February 1893 his beloved sister, Alice, died in England, where she had been staying with their brother Henry. She and William had been very close, and in her last year they had exchanged many long, honest letters about her condition—she had terminal cancer—and her faith. James admired Alice's honesty and bravery in the face of certain death. In his letters, he indulged in a swarm of pet names for her: "Sweetlington, Sisterkin, my Dearest Darling Alice, *la seule que j'aime*, most kissworthy Alice, you lovely Babe." After visiting with her once, William had written that she was "witty and animated and curious about everything." To his mind, she was a prime example of someone who met life's challenges the way he had urged in his *Principles of Psychology*. "Poor little Alice!" James wrote Henry after her death. "What a life! I can't believe that that imperious will and piercing judgment are snuffed out with the breath."[46]

Alice's painful and extended struggle with her illness and the strength of her faith brought William to his next important essay. In April 1895 he lectured at the Harvard YMCA on the provocative topic "Is Life Worth Living?" He answered unabashedly in the affirmative, urging his audience to trust their religious beliefs, which means, first of all, "to live in the light of them, and to act as if the invisible world which they suggest were real." "Not a victory is gained," he continued, "not a deed of faithfulness or courage is done, except upon maybe." We only live "by risking our persons from one hour to another," and it is "all a question of 'maybe.'"[47]

James here again championed the robust, active individual who did not avoid the harshest challenges. If this life be not a real fight, he counseled, in which something is "eternally gained for the universe by success," it is no more than a "game of private theatricals from which one may withdraw at will." But, "if it feels like a real fight—as if there were something really wild in the universe which we, with all our idealities and faithfulness, are needed to redeem," we have to bravely confront it. Our nature is adapted, he continued, to live in such "a half-wild, half-saved universe."[48] It is not just choosing that makes us human but the fact that we have evolved with the tools to confront this dangerous, unpredictable world head-on, not to avoid it. This attitude is what he so admired in his sister, Alice, whose example he urged on any who doubted that life was worth living.

James followed this lecture with one of his most popular, "The Will to Believe," first delivered to the Yale Philosophical Club. It was, as he put it, a "justification of faith" (not a defense of the Protestant "justification *by* faith"), that is, of "our right to adopt a believing attitude in religious matters." Describing what he later elaborated in his theory of pragmatism, he argued that what matters is whether one's hypothesis about belief is "alive" or "dead." Religion, properly conceived, can enliven an individual's embrace of a unique opportunity. If religion is "alive" to someone, he or she acts on it. "He who refuses to embrace a unique opportunity," James wrote, "loses the prize as surely as if he tried and failed."[49]

So, why should one believe in religion? Recall, he reminded his audience, that "science says things are." "Morality says some things are better than other things," while religion says, "the best things are the more eternal things, the overlapping things, the things in the universe that throw the last stone" and have "the final word." Of course, one's faith might prove illusory, but "dupery for dupery, what proof is there that dupery through hope is so much worse than dupery through fear?"[50] By obstinately believing that God exists, he concluded, we do the universe the deepest service we can.[51]

In the summer of 1896 James collected this and other essays dating to the early 1880s in *The Will to Believe*. In the book's preface, he defined his current philosophical position as "radical empiricism." "Empiricism," because one's most assured conclusions are always liable to change as based on new experience. And "radical," because one is open to the possibility that the world might not be at all unified but pluralistic, a place different people saw and experienced in different ways, a fact that provided the best rationale for a truly democratic polity.

James exemplified this belief in a letter to a devout Christian correspondent in which he confessed that religion interested him more than anything else, even though he often had the sense of "a strange shyness of closing my hand on any definite symbols that might be too restrictive." But "I shall work out my destiny," he promised. As a mediator between scientific agnosticism and the religious world, he predicted, "I may be more useful than if I were myself a positive Christian."[52]

The Gifford Lectures

The opportunity to act as such a mediator came in the late 1890s when the University of Edinburgh invited James to give the prestigious Gifford Lectures in Natural Religion. At first, he declined, on account of his health, and recommended his colleague Josiah Royce, who was subsequently invited. The university renewed its offer to James, however, for a later date, and this time he obliged. He was asked to give ten lectures over six weeks in 1899–1900, and another series in 1900–1901. He immediately began to consider a suitable topic.

He eventually lit on "The Varieties of Religious Experience," a topic that arose in part from his reconsideration of his father's religious writings, his own growing belief that scientific knowledge could not be circumvented, and more immediately, a remarkable spiritual experience he had had in the summer of 1898.

He had been vacationing near Lake Placid in the Adirondack Mountains and had hiked all day, climbing Mount Marcy, New York's highest peak. He returned to camp to join his friends. Long after they were asleep, he later wrote to his wife, Alice, he remained awake. That night turned out to be one of the "most memorable of all my memorable experiences."[53] "The influences of Nature, the wholesomeness of the people round me, the good Pauline [Pauline Goldmark, a young woman whom he adored], the thought of you and the children, dear Harry on the wave [his son, Henry, nineteen, going overseas], the problem of the Edinburgh lectures, all fermented in me till it became a regular *Walpurgis nacht*."[54]

He had wandered into the forest, where the streaming moonlight lit things up in magical checkered play. It seemed to him as if the marvel of all nature met in his breast with "the moral gods of the inner life." At the same time, he recognized both the inhuman remoteness of that life and its intense appeal, its promise of everlasting freshness as well as of its antiquity and decay, all whirled inexplicably together. "It was," he concluded, "one of the happiest lonesome nights of my existence."[55]

This was a religious experience comparable to Emerson's when, crossing a bare common at twilight, he had become a "transparent eye-ball" who saw all and felt assuredly that he was "part or particle of God." Or like that of Thoreau on top of Mount Katahdin in the wilderness of Maine, where he had seen "Matter, vast, terrific." "What is this Titan that has possession of me?" Thoreau asked. "Talk of mysteries!—Think of our life in nature—daily to be shown matter, to come in contact with it,—rocks, trees, wind on our cheeks! the *solid* earth! the *actual* world! The *common sense! Contact! Contact! Who* are we? *Where* are we?"[56] Transcendentalists like Emerson and Thoreau, and Swedenborgians like James's father would assuredly have recognized James's experience as an encounter with the divine.

The Gifford Lectures were now constantly on his mind. In the fall of 1898 he wrote a friend that he meant them to be on "the psychology of the religious consciousness, in its developed state," a veritable science of religions rather than a philosophy of religion.[57] At the same time, he had worked up another lecture, "On a Certain Blindness," which pointed to the catholicity he would demonstrate in his Gifford series.[58] Here one sees more clearly where he would go when he considered the political implications of his philosophy, the importance of democracy, given the significance of individual experience. The practical consequence of this view, he explained, "is the well-known democratic respect for the sacredness of individuality—is, at any rate, the outward tolerance of whatever is not itself intolerant," not any state- or culturally imposed religious doctrine.[59]

But James was not quite ready to pen the lectures. In July 1899 he had lost his way on an Adirondack trail and hiked for many more hours than he had anticipated. This exacerbated an occasional problem he had with his heart—after this episode he had frequent "acute thoracic distress"—and under doctor's orders he retreated to the spas of Europe to regain some strength. Edinburgh pushed the lectures back another year. Finally, after several months of cogitation, James began to outline what he would say. He knew for sure that he would not speak about religious institutions but rather religious feelings and religious impulses.

Those in attendance who thought that he would treat the subject of religion traditionally were disappointed. He was not there to talk about ecclesiology or theology, which he associated with "second-hand religious life." Instead, true to his growing belief that scientific inquiry was central to his investigation (as it would be to his budding formulation of pragmatism), he wanted to talk about the original, firsthand experiences that set the patterns of religious feeling.[60]

He would treat religious experiences as if they were hypotheses and investigate where they deductively led. He wanted to know the *practical* results of religious emotion. "By their fruits ye shall know them, not by their roots," he proclaimed. Unsurprisingly, given his continuing interest in Edwards, he cited his *Treatise Concerning the Religious Affections*. Sounding, too, like the young Emerson of the "Divinity School Address" (or his own father railing at the shortcomings of the Swedenborgian church), he complained that churches lived on secondhand tradition, while the founders of every true religion owed their power to the fact of their direct personal experience with the divine. In his lectures, James would address this "personal religion pure and simple," and at the end he hoped to have outlined a prospectus for his science of religions.[61]

In his second lecture James considered what the "divine" in fact was. For him, it was not a superhuman person but the immanent divinity in things, the essentially spiritual structure of the universe, a notion that Edwards had broached similarly in his *End for Which God Created the World*. James recalled his ecstatic moments in the Adirondacks a few years before and claimed that there is a state of mind known to religious people, but to no other, in which the will to assert themselves and hold their own has been displaced by a willingness "to close [their] mouths and be as nothing in the floods and waterspouts of God," what Edwards had described in his "personal Narrative" as being "rapt and swallowed up in God."[62]

In another lecture, James made his famous distinction between the once-born (healthy souls) and the twice-born (sick souls). The first are essentially optimistic, ebullient personalities who, when unhappiness occurs, positively refuse to let it overwhelm them. The others become depressed and melancholy and always live "in darkness and apprehension." These are people who look at the world and see only evil, engendering a consequent sadness and moral paralysis. Such individuals need faith, for without it, humanity is "a set of people living on a frozen lake surrounded by cliffs from which there is no escape, yet knowing that little by little the ice is melting."[63]

The relief from such quiet desperation lay in the possibility of conversion, to be born again and see the world differently. Such a life change occurs in the "hot place in a man's consciousness," where resides the chief set of ideas that animates him, the "*habitual center of his energy*." James returned to Edwards to emphasize this point, using the theologian's own conversion experience as printed in Sereno Edwards Dwight's *Life of President Edwards*. "Self-surrender has been and always must be regarded as the vital turning point of the religious life," James claimed.[64] For the twice-born individual, there are two lives, the natural and the spiritual, but one must lose the first before one may experience the other.

Now working in a fury, James completed the first set of lectures, which were very well received, and homesick for his summer home in Chocorua, New Hampshire, sailed for Boston shortly thereafter. Having another year to compose the second series, he worked more expeditiously. The first five of his second set of lectures, on saintliness and its value, are crucial to understanding James's social ethic. In them, he takes up directly how religious experience might influence one's actions. As he put it, belief has to have social efficacy, as it had in the life of missionary David Brainerd, whose diary and biography Edwards published and whom he cited frequently in his lectures.

When one is twice-born like Brainerd—a "saint" in the Puritans' parlance—one knows a larger life than that lived in self-absorption. One knows that a religious feeling to which one wholly submits inspires one's life. One experiences an immense elation and freedom as "confining self-hood melts down," and there is an ensuing shift of "the emotional center towards loving and harmonious affections."[65] Sin is selfishness; and grace is the movement from self toward selflessness, which true to his own Protestant heritage, James memorably urged on his audience.

He went on to stress the practical, transformative effects of such belief. In what might have been a jibe at the Gilded Age's robber barons, he wrote, "Lives based on having are less free than lives based either on doing or on being." In political terms, the implications were clear. The active religious life is at the heart of "the mystery of democracy, or sentiment of the equality before God of all his creatures," he continued. But it has to be a well-regulated democracy and should not degenerate into a mere meritocracy. In a message that smacks of James's disgust at the nation's renewed colonialism in the wake of the recent Spanish-American War, he asserted that "what we now need to discover in the social realm is the moral equivalent of war; something heroic that will speak to men as universally as war does, and yet will be as compatible with their spiritual selves as war has proved itself to be incompatible."[66] Later in his life, in 1910, he prepared a talk on this very subject that became one of his most reprinted essays.

James acknowledged that different individuals experienced true religion in different ways, and that all such encounters with the divine should be considered genuine and valued equally, even if they could not be explained with absolute certainty. The marks of such true religious experience were four and worth comparing to what Edwards had urged in his *Religious Affections*. Such an experience is *ineffable*, defying easy description; *noetic*, offering a new kind of knowledge; *transient*, never lasting for very long; and *passive*, as if a person "were grasped and held by a superior power."[67] James then offered excerpts from a lengthy list of firsthand accounts from a wide array of people: Alfred, Lord Tennyson; Ralph Waldo Trine; Walt Whitman; Emerson; various Hindu and Buddhist witnesses; Saint Teresa; Ignatius of Loyola; George Fox; Jakob Böhme; and Leo Tolstoy, among others.

So, James asked after this bravura recitation, "can we invoke the mystic range of consciousness as authoritative?" Yes, he replied, mystical states are authoritative *over those who experience them*, and their existence "absolutely overthrows the pretension of non-mystical states to be the sole and ultimate dictators of what we may believe."[68] The experience of such mystical states also trumps the specious claims of formal theology. We must conclude, he argued, that any attempt to demonstrate the truth of direct religious experience by purely intellectual processes is absolutely hopeless. Faith, James was saying, can only be known by each individual *in his or her own way* and is finally to be judged by what difference it makes in a person's life.

James reminded his audience that, as the French mathematician and theologian Blaise Pascal had said, belief in God comprises a wager: one should bet "yes, God exists," for one loses nothing if he does not but claims an invaluable reward if he does. This complemented James's own insistence that, "No fact in human nature is more characteristic than its willingness to live on a chance." "Who knows," he mused in his final lecture, "whether the faithfulness of individuals here below to their own poor over-beliefs may not actually help God in turn to be more effectively faithful to his own greater tasks."[69]

Fruits of the Metaphysical Club

As with the Transcendental Club, that small group of disaffected young Unitarians who met for a few years in the late 1830s to talk about religion and philosophy, Cambridge's Metaphysical Club was never formally constituted. Years later, Charles Sanders Peirce recalled that "it was in the earliest seventies [in fact, in January 1872] that a knot of us young men in Old Cambridge, calling ourselves, half-ironically, half-defiantly, 'The Metaphysical Club' . . . used to meet, sometimes in my study, sometimes in that of William James."[70] Regulars included the law professor Oliver Wendell Holmes, the historian John Fiske, and the philosopher Francis Ellington Abbot. The implicit leader and oldest member of the group was Chauncey Wright, a stalwart empiricist who rejected any proposition that could not be verified scientifically. Writing to Charles Eliot Norton, the younger Henry James reported, tongue in cheek, "[Holmes], my brother, and other long-headed youths have combined to form a metaphysical club, where they wrangle grimly and stick to the question." Not being inclined to that sort of social gathering, he wryly observed, "It gives me a headache merely to know of it."[71]

The one who most often stirred and seasoned the club's bubbling cauldron of ideas was Peirce, who had graduated from Harvard in 1859 and entered the Lawrence Scientific School just before James.[72] He had a brilliant mathematical mind and developed what is now recognized as the field of semiotics. Peirce subsequently worked for the United States Coast Survey as a gravimetrician (someone who measures gravity to learn about the shape of the earth and its interior). Among the cognoscenti, he was legendary. In 1877 one English mathematician called him "the greatest living logician, and the second man since Aristotle who had added to the subject something material."[73] But Peirce was also bristling, prickly, and frequently in ill health, suffering from a painful facial neuralgia, for which he took opium. In spite of Peirce's peculiarities, though, William James observed to his brother Henry after Peirce had dined with Henry in Paris, "I like him very much," for "he is a man of genius."[74]

Peirce's pioneering work in semiotics was not appreciated for years. Immediately noticed by club members in the 1870s, however, was his contribution to philosophical analysis that came to be called pragmatism. James pondered the method for years and first publicly announced it in 1898 at a lecture at Berkeley and then codified it in his book *Pragmatism*, published in 1907.[75] He was thinking about it in his Gifford Lectures, too, with his emphasis on a critical science of religions discoverable through empirical inquiry.

Peirce thus described the movement's chief proposition: "What a man really believes is what he would be ready to act upon." Thereafter, he tried to "weave that truth in with others which he had made out for himself," so as to make a consistent doctrine of cognition. James later refined the definition: "the whole function of thinking" is but "one step in the production of habits of action."[76]

Peirce had borrowed the term *pragmatism* from Kant, who thought "pragmatic" belief was one among many ways of believing. But Peirce argued that it was in fact the *only* way to know something. The chief questions to ask about a proposition are these: What is an idea worth? What are you willing to risk for it? How do you think something will result if you hold a certain belief, and what would you wager on that? Peirce also challenged the notion that any individual can completely comprehend reality, for the reality of something is the sum of what *all* minds think about it, an idea that also underlay James's *Varieties.* "The opinion which is fated to be ultimately agreed to by all who investigate, is what we mean by the truth, and the object represented in this opinion is the real."[77] The connection between such a notion and James's later championing of radical empiricism is clear.

Peirce, too, understood the political implications of his statements. As though interrogating one of Emerson's propositions about self-reliance, he observed that "the question whether the *genus homo* has any existence except as individuals," is the question "whether there is anything of any more dignity, worth, and importance than individual happiness, individual aspirations, individual life." And whether the community is to be considered an end in itself is "the most fundamental practical question in regard to every public institution the constitution of which we have it in our power to influence."[78]

Peirce believed he had answers. One's interests, he continued, should never be limited to one's self. We must not stop at our own fate but must value that of the whole community, for "logic is rooted in the social principle."[79] Soon enough, James, hearing echoes of his father's Swedenborgianism, wove such thoughts into his own writings and introduced Peirce's formulations to a much larger audience.

James's growing commitment to this new philosophical method gained a boost when he was asked to speak in Concord at the centenary of Emerson's birth in 1903. He reread his godfather's entire oeuvre and, in volumes that still exist, marked his favorite passages, including some from Emerson's Harvard lectures on "The Natural History of Intellect," that already had shown him moving toward what became pragmatism. After several false starts, James finally focused on Emerson as a champion of individuality. "The matchless eloquence with which Emerson proclaimed the sovereignty of the living individual," James observed, "electrified and emancipated his generation, and this bugle blast will doubtless be regarded by future critics as the soul of his message."[80]

Pragmatism

In the late fall, aging now and ever more convinced of the logic of consequence arising from the active soul making order from chance, James enthusiastically signed on for another set of Lowell Lectures. Unsurprisingly, he announced his topic as "Pragmatism." The talks were immensely popular—around five hundred people attended each of the eight lectures—because of the convincing way he was able to frame his topic. James argued that the world is not unified, not singular but pluralistic, "made up of a lot of eaches." He found himself, he admitted, "willing to take the universe to be really dangerous and adventurous, without therefore backing out and crying 'no play.'"

He also was willing, he continued, to acknowledge "that there should be real losses and real losers, and not total preservation of all that is." For that was no matter. "When the cup is poured off," he explained, "the dregs are left behind forever, but the possibility of what is poured off is sweet enough to accept." From looking backward on principles, he wrote, pragmatism shifts the emphasis and looks forward empirically to facts themselves. The really vital question for us all is, "What is the world going to be? What is life eventually to make of itself?"[81]

These were profoundly moral but also political questions, ones that would resonate in the life and work of such "muckrakers" and other reformers like Lincoln Steffens, Ida Tarbell, Upton Sinclair, Jacob Riis, Ida B. Wells, and W. E. B. Du Bois, men and women who at the turn of the century brought to light widespread political corruption at both the local and national levels: intolerable working conditions for children as well as adults, widespread racial injustice, collusion among the nation's trusts, and the horrific conditions of the nation's urban poor. James challenged mere compliance with or acquiescence to the hierarchical and bureaucratic forces that stifled true democracy. Pragmatism encouraged principled action for social justice and mutual respect among citizens of all races, genders, or points of view, even as it discouraged mere resignation or, worse, resort to violence.

James distinguished between two chief ways to view the world. If one is a rationalist, he explained, one adheres to abstract and eternal principles, like his Harvard colleague philosopher Josiah Royce. If one is an empiricist, one is a "lover of facts in all their crude variety." Another way to phrase this is to think of two temperaments. There are the "tender-minded," who are "rationalistic, (going by 'principles'), intellectualistic, idealistic, optimist, religious, free-willed, monistic, and dogmatical." And there are the "tough-minded," who are "empiricist (going by 'facts'), sensationalistic, materialistic, pessimistic, irreligious, fatalistic, pluralistic, and skeptical."[82] He presented pragmatism as a mediating philosophy, to resolve the conflict between the two temperaments, and religion and science. Pragmatism also encouraged democratic polity, for it demanded free and open inquiry of all members of a community in the pursuit of reasonable and equitable solutions to social ills.

Early in the series, James gave his friend Peirce his due as the progenitor of the movement.[83] It was he, James explained, who in Metaphysical Club meetings had claimed that, to attain perfect clearness in one's thoughts of an object, one need only consider what conceivable effects of a practical kind the object may involve—what sensations one is to expect from it, and what reactions one must prepare. One's conception of these effects, James explained, "whether immediate or remote," is one's entire conception of the object. The pragmatist thus turns away from abstractions and closed systems and "toward concreteness and adequacy, towards facts, towards action and power," working toward solutions to the world's problems, be they social or political in nature.[84]

For James, the "true" was whatever proved itself congruent with how and what a person already believed. A pragmatist's only test of probable truth is what works best to help him or her keep going, allowing him to act, "what fits every part of life best and combines with the collectivity of experience's demands, nothing being omitted." Philosophy regarded in this way is not some abstract, armchair study but a guide to action, to living the best life. True ideas, he believed, were those that one could assimilate, validate, corroborate, and verify; false ideas, those that one cannot. "Truth is made," James explained, "just as health, wealth, and strength are made, in the course of experience." Truth *happens* to an idea, he opined. "It *becomes* true, is *made* true by events."[85]

Such talk was anathema to strict monists but welcome tonic for those in need of a stimulant to acting on life's stage, particularly for the growing band of reformers who addressed myriad contemporary problems caused by industrialization, urbanization, immigration, racial inequality, and political corruption. "I am against bigness and greatness in all their forms," James had written. "The bigger the unit you deal with," he continued, "the hollower, the more brutal, the more mendacious is the life displayed."[86] James believed that "our acts, our turning places, where we seek to make ourselves and grow are the parts of the world to which we are closest," and that could mean in urban ghettos as well as on Wall Street. Why not then take these acts at their face value? Why might they not be "the actual turning-places and growing-places which they seem to be"? Why might they not be "the workshop of being, where we catch fact in the making?"[87]

This applied to the most insignificant as well as the most profound propositions, including whether to value religious faith. James now returned what he had offered in the conclusion of his Gifford Lectures. On pragmatic principles, he counseled, if the hypothesis of God works satisfactorily for someone, in the widest sense of the word, it *is* true for that individual. James no doubt had his father in mind when he wrote this, a man for whom the spiritual world had "worked," had been so "true" that this unshakeable belief gave his life profound significance. But James also acknowledged that for individuals to believe that they can make for themselves any life they imagine, as Emerson had suggested in his earlier essays, was unrealistic. One could best face the harsh realities that intrude into each life as self-aware individuals sharing in the collective experience that Peirce counseled.

James's lectures appeared in June 1907 as *Pragmatism: A New Name for Some Old Ways of Thinking*. The book went through four printings before the end of the year; but, to James's disappointment, it met with a mixed reception from the professional community, who complained about its lack of logical rigor and its breezy, colloquial style. James was puzzled by what he took to be their misunderstanding of his purpose—it was not "a philosophy got up for the use of engineers, electricians and doctors" but grew "from a more subtle and delicate theoretic analysis of the function of knowing" for *all* people, including those who were the subject of the muckrakers' investigative reporting or the urban poor that ministers of the "Social Gospel" worked tirelessly to serve.[88]

James's lectures reveal how the world had changed since he had begun to write in the wake of the Civil War. Now, it was more and more defined by large-scale industry and transformative inventions—electricity, automobiles, phonography, X-rays, telephones, and moving pictures, to name some of the most memorable—and where efficiency and usefulness mattered most. Much of this displeased him because of how it seemingly diminished the power of individuals to effect change. "I am against all big organizations," he once wrote, "national ones first and foremost," and "all big successes and big results," and in favor of "the eternal forces of truth which always work in the individual."

Not that he dismissed heroic action as impossible, however. In 1897 in a speech at the unveiling of Augustus Saint-Gaudens's monument to Colonel Robert Gould Shaw, who had led the Massachusetts Fifty-Fourth Regiment in the Civil War and had died in an assault on Fort Wagner, South Carolina, James eloquently praised the soldier's valor. But he also opined that a great democracy is one not so much saved by wars as that in which "the civic genius of the people does the saving day by day, by acts without external picturesqueness; by speaking, writing, voting reasonably; by smiting corruption swiftly; by good temper between parties; by the people knowing true men when they meet them, and preferring them as leaders to rabid partisans or empty quacks."[89]

The United States as a political entity was undergoing great change, too, for by the 1890s, the continent fully settled, it had become an imperialist power outside its geographical boundaries. At the end of the Spanish-American War, the country annexed Hawaii, Puerto Rico, and Guam and gained temporary control of the Philippines and a foothold in Cuba. James was particularly incensed at the country's behavior in the Philippines, where President William McKinley suppressed the local independence movement of the Tagalog people as he made the islands an American protectorate.[90] James wrote angrily that McKinley was "crushing out the sacredest thing in this human world," the "attempt of a people long enslaved to attain the possession of itself, to organize its own laws and government, to be free to follow its internal destinies according to its own ideals."[91] But in a phrase that was on everyone's lips, it seemed the "manifest destiny" of the United States to expand its power and influence in just such ways, even if James and other lonely voices decried the blatant racism that underlay it.

The nation also faced new challenges as capital and labor came into conflict that more frequently led to frightening violence. The Haymarket riots and bombing in Chicago in 1886, subsequently punctuated by eight anarchists' conviction for conspiracy on trumped up charges; the Homestead strike in 1892 in Carnegie's Pennsylvania steel mills that culminated in a fierce battle between strikers and private security forces; the Pullman strike in 1894 in Illinois, which pitted labor organizer Eugene Debs and the American Railway Union against the Midwest's rail monopolies after residents of the company town of Pullman had their wages lowered without a subsequent reduction in rents: everywhere workers sought more autonomy, the right to shape the conditions under which they labored, and to negotiate fair rewards for their work. Class divisions ripped apart the nation as capitalists defended and sought to increase their already vast fortunes.

James fashioned his philosophy as a response to such social disruption as well as to the rapid spread of philosophical relativism. In a lecture delivered at the University of California at Berkeley, in 1911, his Harvard colleague George Santayana accurately described his colleague's importance. William James, he averred, "had a prophetic sympathy with the dawning sentiments of the age." His way of thinking and feeling, he continued, "represented in a measure the whole ultramodern, radical world."[92] In a letter to British writer and social activist H. G. Wells, James himself identified the age's chief problem: "the exclusive worship of the bitch-Goddess SUCCESS." Rather than confront what James viewed as unconstitutional intervention by the government, most troublingly by the federal injunction to end the Pullman strike, the average citizen continued to "breed excuses from his general fund of optimism and respect for expediency." The result was a "callousness to abstract justice" that had become "the sinister feature . . . of our U. S. Civilization," at the expense of the working poor and otherwise socially disadvantaged.[93]

Though these years, though suffering from more and more frequent heart pains, James continued to plan his volume on radical empiricism. When Manchester University in England invited him to deliver a series of eight lectures, he enthusiastically accepted. His talks became his next book, *A Pluralistic Universe*, published in 1909. In it, James reviewed the development of philosophy in the last half century. "Let empiricism," he declared, "once become associated with religion, as hitherto, through some strange misunderstanding, it has been associated with irreligion, and I believe a new era of religion as well as of philosophy will . . . begin." He continued to champion a scientific explanation of faith, one that utilized "hypotheses, and deductions from these, controlled by sense observations and analogies with what we know elsewhere."[94] "All that my *pluralism* contends for," James wrote a friend in 1910, "is that there is nowhere extant a complete gathering up of the universe in *one* focus, either of knowledge, power, or purpose."[95]

Seemingly unable to shake his father's ghost, however, in his last years James returned to the study of mystical states, now touting the work of Gustav Fechner, a German psychologist who believed in a cosmic consciousness.[96] "Instead of believing our life to be fed at the breasts of the greater life," James went on, "we habitually treat whatever lies outside of our life as so much slag and ashes of life only."[97] "I firmly disbelieve," he wrote, "that our human experience is the highest form of experience extant in the universe." He ended with a marvelous image. "I believe rather," he continued, "that we stand in much the same relation to the whole of the universe as our canine and feline pets do to the whole of human life." They inhabit our drawing rooms and libraries. They take part in scenes of whose significance they have no inkling. "They are merely tangent to curves of history the beginnings and ends and forms of which pass wholly beyond their ken." So, James concluded, "we are tangent to the wider life of things."[98] His audience loved this.

Early in 1910, learning that his brother Henry, now an internationally acclaimed novelist, was ill with some sort of nervous disorder at his home in Rye, England, James and his wife, Alice, immediately booked passage. But William himself was in decline, suffering from much shortness of breath and having trouble with any sort of exertion. He diagnosed his brother's condition as a serious nervous breakdown and stayed with him into the summer. But by the end of his visit, he himself had become such an invalid that he had to be carried onto the transatlantic steamer.

Sailing to Quebec rather than to Boston so that he could travel overland to see his beloved White Mountains, on August 19 he arrived at Chocorua, New Hampshire, where his family had long owned a summer home. His condition worsened. The family administered digitalis and morphine, but it was clear that he was dying. A week later, with Alice cradling his head, William James passed into that unknown about which he had so passionately wondered ever since a boy at his father's side.

Pluralism and Democracy

William James's contributions to the American experiment were manifold.[99] Like Emerson he upheld the sanctity of each individual and argued his or her duty to make a valuable contribution to the common good. He moved Emerson's self-reliance in new directions for the twentieth century, particularly through his insistence that the good citizen has to embrace outward action that furthers democratic society, a goal urged as well by another estimable pragmatist, his contemporary John Dewey, and other reformers such as Ida B. Wells and James's former student Du Bois, who wrote that James was one of Harvard's transformational leaders who, "unshackled in thought and custom," were "beating back bars of ignorance and particularism and prejudice."[100]

As James's colleague Royce put it, he was the country's "national philosopher" because "certain characteristic aspects of our national civilization" found their voice in him. James stood, Royce continued, for an important "stage in our national self-consciousness" because he understood, shared, and also "transcended the American spirit," not shying away from the sometimes difficult challenges that citizenship presented.[101] James believed, Royce suggested, that people were responsible not only for their lives but for those of others and were obligated to act in the service of a democratic ideal that respected all individuals, no matter what their gender, race, or social position.

Santayana, writing that same year, suggested that James's "way of thinking and feeling" represented "the true America."[102] James loved the concrete, the particular, the individual, and the ways that the various pieces fit together to make American democracy work. He regarded experience as the key to truth and meaning and believed that the essence of the conscious life lay in its practical, active nature, in its creative reaction to whatever good and bad the universe threw at one. "Intelligence" was nothing less than practical adjustment to the world's undeniable facts. To a moral person at the turn of the twentieth century, this also meant having an awareness of the world's manifold ills and a willingness to work to cure them.

However, if one makes certain choices in response to a given situation, what makes one pick *those* choices instead of others? If temperament is the reason, how does one person's temperament get to be what it is? This is the same question, in modern dress, that Jonathan Edwards had addressed in his *Freedom of the Will* and that Emerson had broached in his essay "Experience." James answered by championing pluralism. As long as each individual tested his or her notions of meaning and truth by their empirical consequences, they had to be respected.

For James, life was a process of continuous growth through experience; one's actions defined and transformed one. Each person is a cocreator of the universe and is born anew each moment as new experience presents itself. Like Emerson, James distrusted institutions and systems. But for him, the individual was not a transcendental absolute but someone who helps that absolute realize itself in this life as one worked alongside all other people to affect its incarnation. In a democracy, belief and action are inextricably bound. Life demands that an individual decides, chooses this or that. And every such decision moves the known universe in a new direction, determined not by Edwards's transcendent deity or Emerson's Oversoul but realized through the active life.

James thus helped midwife a modern, secular world. He championed a philosophy of action, of choice. For him, life was an endless flow of experience, and the universe a set of innumerable possibilities among which avoidance as well as acceptance was itself a form of response. One had to trust instinct, to have faith, to take a chance: not to do so was not to be fully alive. Such a philosophy could not but influence one's interactions with other beings. One accepted one's fellows as equals, acknowledging in them what James most treasured, self-worth, even if those others chose to live their lives differently through a different set of beliefs.

William James foresaw the contingency and ambiguity that came to define the twentieth century in physical and spiritual terms. His world became that of William Faulkner, Gertrude Stein, W. E. B. Du Bois, Pablo Picasso, Sigmund Freud, Igor Stravinsky, Alfred Einstein, and Werner Heisenberg. He glimpsed a brave new world and urged mankind not to fear but to embrace it, for even without the palliative of certainty, to live, to accept the universe, involves risk that defines one's humanity.

4
John Rawls
THE SEARCH FOR TWENTIETH-CENTURY JUSTICE

Harvard, 1960s

William James would have found a kindred spirit in John Rawls, one of his successors in Harvard's Philosophy Department, housed in appropriately named Emerson Hall. Always concerned with the morality of international warfare, Rawls was an early and vocal critic of the Vietnam War, which he regarded as unjust. So, too, James had strongly condemned American aggression, in his case, in the Spanish-American War (1898), when for the first time the United States annexed territory outside its continental borders. The widespread American war fever disgusted him, as did his belief that business interests, who now exercised power in foreign policy, had trumped up the conflict. His outrage at this jingoism eventually found its way into one of his most popular works, *The Moral Equivalent of War*.[1]

Rawls himself might have written this piece, for in the 1960s he objected to the United States' involvement in war in Vietnam on similar principles. In the mid-1960s, realizing that there was little hope that President Lyndon Johnson soon would end the fighting, Rawls and other philosophers and ethical theorists, including Michael Walzer, Robert Nozick, Thomas Nagel, T. M. Scanlon, and Ronald Dworkin, formed the Society for Ethical and Legal Philosophy, which met monthly in Cambridge and New York to consider how philosophy might be brought to bear on contemporary social problems, an indication of the growing role of the academy as a distinctive and powerful element in the fabric of American culture.

Among other things, Rawls was deeply troubled by the then compulsory military service for men up to the age of twenty-six, the selective service "draft." By 1969, some members of the American Philosophical Society decided on an academic intervention in national policy and formed the Society for Philosophy and Public Affairs to discuss solutions to problems of war, civic responsibility to the state, and the nature and justification for civil disobedience. Rawls was a primary member of this group and in their meetings began to work out the details of what later became part of his major contribution to political philosophy.

At Harvard in 1969 he was most concerned by the controversial "2-s" deferment, which exempted college students in good standing from military service and which he considered unfair. Because professors assigned grades and helped compute class rankings that local draft boards could use in making their decisions, this gave them an inordinate amount of power over a young man's future. The rule favored those fortunate enough to attend college and thus implicitly the children of the wealthy over those who did not have the same resources to prepare their children for college. Rawls believed that if young men were going to be forced to go to war, all Americans of the requisite age should share the burden. If all eligible young men were not needed for military duty, the necessary number could be determined by lottery.

Rawls recruited seven colleagues from the Philosophy Department, including Hilary Putnam and Stanley Cavell, and eight from Political Science, including Stanley Hoffmann, Michael Walzer, and Harvey Mansfield. At two faculty meetings late in that year and early the next, they proposed a motion asking faculty to express opposition to the deferment. "Conscription," Rawls wrote, "is a drastic interference with the liberties of a few in society and cannot be justified by any needs less compelling than those of national security." The present system, he continued, "grants deferments on a large scale for weak reasons of social interest [and as a result] the hardships and risks of compulsory service fall disproportionately on the poor, the less intelligent, and the less well educated."[2]

To Rawls's disappointment, the motion was defeated by more cautious and conservative faculty, encouraged to do so by Harvard president Nathan Pusey. By the end of 1969, however, the United States initiated on a national scale just such a draft lottery system, vindicating Rawls's position but eventually troubling him in a different way as he realized that a voluntary military, as opposed to universal conscription, ruined the dream of equal citizenship he sought. But there was still the larger problem of the Vietnam War, only the latest of several cataclysmic events that marked the twentieth century. During these years the American experiment had accelerated by every measure: population, demographics, wealth, international power and prestige, and transformative technologies had been introduced like television, the computer, and space travel. But by 1970, despite such phenomenal growth, the country had been challenged by three international wars, a Great Depression, and both peaceful and violent agitation for civil rights.

Since World War II, the United States had grown tremendously. A state bureaucracy that had been nonexistent in Jonathan Edwards's day but increasingly intrusive by William James's time was now omnipresent, its immense power underpinned by what President Dwight Eisenhower called a vast "military-industrial complex." As a result, even though Americans remained overwhelmingly Christian, they increasingly looked to state institutions to explain and expand matters of justice, the demands of citizenship, and national purpose.

Rawls's personal journey, from faith and confidence in the truth and efficacy of Christianity to a lifelong engagement with justification for a liberal democratic consensus, epitomized by then unstoppable secularization. How did Rawls navigate this change? Like so many of his fellow countrymen, the experience of war—World War II, Korea, and Vietnam—challenged his belief in a God as the arbiter of justice and made him turn instead to the reasonableness of citizens themselves.

Witness Rawls in the spring of 1969 confronting the Vietnam War. The trouble began on an early spring day, April 9, when Harvard's classes were in session.[3] The previous evening the university chapter of Students for a Democratic Society (SDS), a politically left student activist movement, had met to plan their spring agenda. For months, they had tried to educate students, faculty, and staff about pressing social issues on campus. In particular, they sought to abolish the Reserve Officers' Training Corps (ROTC) program because it implicitly condoned the war in Vietnam and end all of Harvard's existing contracts with the United States military. The SDS also objected to some of the university's social and economic policies, particularly a recent increase in rents on properties it controlled and its plan to demolish lower-class homes and housing units in neighborhoods into which Harvard intended to expand.

That evening, the SDS membership agreed on the issues they wished to press but were divided on how they would achieve their goals. More radical students made plans to seize University Hall, occupied by the deans of the college, the next day at noon and prevailed in the debate. They cranked up their mimeograph machines and by breakfast the morning of the planned takeover delivered notices to all the university dining halls encouraging students to lend their support.

Shortly before noon, and before a crowd of several hundred curious bystanders, several-score students marched up the granite steps of University Hall. Through a bullhorn, one of them reiterated the demands settled on the previous evening and condemned the Harvard Corporation (the university's governing body) for being unwilling even to meet and entertain the students' proposals. At noon, some fifty demonstrators entered through the unlocked doors and began evicting the occupants, including deans and their support staff.

The majority of the university employees left voluntarily; others were literally carried out. Dean of the Faculty Franklin Ford was the last to leave. When he warned the occupiers that they were obstructing free passage to members of the university community, he was told, "Shut up, you pig. Get out. This building is occupied." The demonstrators then secured the doors with chains, began rifling through desks and files to liberate documents about ROTC or other of the university's activities, and urged those in the crowd outside, now numbering about eight hundred, to join them. Some did, but the majority remained onlookers, split over supporting or condemning the unprecedented action. Soon, the crowd had swelled to two thousand.

Throughout the afternoon and early evening, the deans huddled with an anxious and angry President Nathan Pusey in his home on Quincy Street just outside Harvard Yard. To the dismay of some of his advisors but with the support of Dean Ford, the president decided to clear the building. By midnight, municipal police, armed with shields and batons, gathered near Memorial Hall, just outside the Yard. They awaited six buses filled with two hundred state policemen wearing boots, jodhpurs, and shining blue riot helmets.

Just before 5:00 a.m., still in darkness, the buses carrying the state troopers entered the Yard. The municipal police cordoned the hall's perimeter against the huge crowd of students who had gathered throughout the night. The state police massed near the entrances as dean of the college, Fred Glimp, told the occupiers that they had five minutes to leave the building or face arrest. At precisely 5:00 a.m., the state police used a battering ram and chain cutters to open the doors of University Hall. They raced in, pushing and clubbing students as they went, driving them together so that they had nowhere to go, many nursing bloody wounds. The troopers pushed, kicked, or pulled the demonstrators out of the building and into waiting paddy wagons and buses for the ride to arraignment.

It was over in half an hour. One hundred ninety-six people were booked at Cambridge District Court. Forty-eight were injured seriously enough to require medical attention, mainly for scalp wounds, concussions, and fractures. As daylight came, a shaken university community was aghast at the violence that its administration had condoned. Among these was professor of philosophy John Rawls, who was already on record as a critic of the draft and a supporter of civil disobedience.[4]

Professor of government Stanley Hoffmann also was among those appalled by the university's response to the occupation. He and department colleague Michael Walzer, both early critics of the Vietnam War, contacted about eighty like-minded faculty, including Nobel Prize–winning biologist George Wald, psychologist Jerome Bruner, economists Wassily Leontief and John Kenneth Galbraith, and Rawls, to decide what to do.

Convening that afternoon, this group rejected a conservative caucus's proposal that urged restraint instead of more protest and a cooling-down period before convening the faculty as a whole. The more liberal group saw matters differently and urged an early meeting of the entire faculty to decide how to address the occupiers' demands as well as the administration's ham-handed handling of the occupation. Rawls carried this request to Dean Ford, and a faculty meeting was set for Friday afternoon. The liberal caucus met again and settled on formal resolutions to bring for debate at the meeting, including support for the removal from campus of ROTC. Rawls hurried off to mimeograph copies of the document to distribute at the meeting.

At the faculty meeting, the liberal caucus prevailed, but subsequent deliberations, meetings, and resolutions continued to occupy the university community for months, including the dropping of criminal charges against the occupiers; the decision to elect of a Committee of Fifteen to investigate the causes of the crisis, decide on appropriate discipline, and recommend changes in faculty governance; and the termination of special arrangements with ROTC.

There also was another problem. Many students, including an African American group, wanted to continue to strike unless they saw swift response to their demands for curricular reform. Part of these students' frustration with the university lay in what they regarded as their courses' irrelevance to contemporary national and world problems. In particular, they sought the establishment of a program in or department of black studies of the sort some other peer institutions had already created.

To its credit, the university formed a committee to work out the details of such a program. At a meeting with prospective African American majors in the evening of that inauspicious day, April 9, this standing committee announced the details of the proposed major. What they heard infuriated African Americans and their supporters because the committee proposed linking the major to some already-established field—Black Studies and History, say, or Black Studies and Political Science. The students thought this insulting, for it implied that the proposed program's courses were not adequate or rigorous enough by themselves to constitute a major. They also objected that the proposal did not include their call for active student participation in the selection of courses and of professors to be hired.

Supporters of the African American group continued to meet over the next two weeks. They selected representatives to present to the faculty an outline of what they considered an acceptable program. To do this, they needed to find professors sympathetic to their cause and willing to move the proposal to the full faculty. They knew where to go to find help: Emerson Hall. There, Professors Rawls and Cavell assisted them in revising their draft into a form suitable for presentation as a motion to the faculty. The two also agreed to introduce and second the students' resolution at the general faculty meeting. Rawls and Cavell worked on the resolution for two days. The final document included what was on most of the students' wish list, save for the proposal that gave students power over faculty appointments, something Rawls and Cavell knew that Harvard's professors would never approve.

Unfortunately, the faculty meeting turned rancorous and divisive and adjourned after passing a motion to defer further discussion of the proposal until the following week. At that next meeting, the faculty finally approved a slightly revised version of the Rawls/Cavell document. Rawls's sponsorship of this important but controversial document epitomized his commitment to justice, fairness, and pluralism, in this case, in his academic community. It was wholly in line with his pathbreaking work-in-progress in moral philosophy.

Becoming a Philosopher

John Bordley Rawls was born on February 21, 1921, in Baltimore, Maryland, the second of five sons of William Lee and Anna Abell Rawls.[5] The Rawls family had southern roots—his paternal grandfather had been a banker in Greenville, North Carolina, who had moved to Baltimore for his health, to be near the Johns Hopkins University hospitals. His maternal grandparents, who had coal and oil holdings in Pennsylvania, were from the Baltimore area.

By the early 1900s, however, whatever wealth the family had owned had been dissipated. Rawls's father never finished high school but eventually educated himself well enough to pass the bar exam. He became a successful corporate lawyer in a long-established Baltimore firm and helped rebuild the family's wealth. He did well enough to purchase a summer cottage across the bay from Mount Desert Island near Blue Hill, Maine, where the family, and later Rawls and his children, spent many summers.

During Rawls's youth his parents took an active interest in local and national politics. His mother was for some time president of the new League of Women Voters in Baltimore and in 1940 worked for Republican Wendell Willkie's presidential campaign. Rawls's father had voted for Woodrow Wilson and approved of the League of Nations. He later supported Franklin Roosevelt and his New Deal programs, until 1937, when the president tried to pack the Supreme Court with six new justices—William Lee Rawls was a stickler for strict constitutional principles. The governor of Maryland thought enough of him to nominate him to the state supreme court, but Rawls declined for health reasons: he suffered from tuberculosis, as had his father.

Illness in the family provided John's most indelible memory from his childhood years. In 1928, he contracted a serious illness. The family doctor told his parents to keep the other children from entering his room until he had reached a diagnosis, but Rawls's brother Bobby sneaked in a few times to keep John company. Soon both boys were gravely ill with what turned out to be diphtheria. Antitoxin was administered. John eventually recovered, but Bobby died. The next year, John contracted pneumonia and infected his brother Tommy. Tragedy repeated itself: he recovered, but his brother did not. Rawls long pondered why his siblings had to die while he was allowed to live, how sheer contingency, something William James would have understood, had played so large a role in his survival.

Early on, Rawls was made aware of social injustice, too, first in the form of racial segregation, for in Baltimore blacks lived in different neighborhoods and attended different schools. All his life he remembered his mother's displeasure that he had made friends with a young black boy and had even visited him in his home in a segregated neighborhood. Similarly, when his family summered in Maine, Rawls recognized how much less well off the year-round residents were. This awakened a lifelong concern with how fortunate he was and how unfortunate were many others because of such matters as race, geography, or occupation.

Rawls attended Baltimore's private Calvert School. He next went to a public junior high school; but after that, in 1935, as was the custom for many of the city's wealthier families, his parents sent him to boarding school, the prestigious Kent School in western Connecticut, an all-boys, Episcopal institution.

Headed by a monk of the Poughkeepsie-based order of the Holy Cross, the Kent School's regimen was strict. Students had to remain on campus at all times and were not allowed even to go into town for movies or refreshments. They were assigned house chores and required to attend religious services six days a week and twice on Sunday. Rawls received high grades and was an active member of the community, joining the varsity football and wrestling teams and playing the trumpet in the school's jazz band. He graduated in 1939 but by his own report he had not been overly happy with the experience. He had not been challenged by the academics.

Like his older brother, William, Rawls next went to Princeton University. He arrived on campus in September 1939, on the cusp of the Second World War. Unlike many of his classmates, he did not enroll in ROTC classes, but he agreed with the majority of his peers that, when push came to shove, the United States would have to support Great Britain in its struggle with Germany. He tried athletics at college, again in the footsteps of his older brother, but he dropped away from both football and wrestling after a year. He joined one of the elite eating clubs, the Ivy, around which his social life revolved. He was unsure of his major and considered art and archaeology before settling on philosophy in his junior year. He recalled that he was only "conventionally religious" until his last two years at college.[6]

With Professor Walter T. Stace, a utilitarian, he studied Immanuel Kant and John Stuart Mill, who became lifelong influences, as did Stace, for whom Rawls wrote his undergraduate honors thesis. Another of Rawls's important instructors was Norman Malcolm, ten years his senior, who had studied with Ludwig Wittgenstein at the University of Cambridge and written his dissertation at Harvard with C. I. Lewis, a well-known phenomenologist. Malcolm's demanding course work challenged and pleased Rawls. When he was a senior he took another course with him, on human evil, in which he studied Plato, Saint Augustine, and Reinhold Niebuhr, among others. Rawls later credited Malcolm with cementing his interest in philosophy. The nature of Malcolm's course indicates that some members of the college's Philosophy Department also were interested in theology, for as yet there was no separate Religion Department.

Malcolm's course on evil moved Rawls to write his senior thesis on "A Brief Inquiry into the Meaning of Sin and Faith: An Interpretation Based on the Concept of Community," a work that remarkably foreshadowed his later interest in moral philosophy.[7] Therein he proposed that a proper ethical attitude had at its center a recognition of the primary importance of persons and the communities in which they lived, and that a compelling ethical vision should have as its end the creation of an inclusive redeemed community.[8] No person was merely a "thing," he insisted, and should never be treated as such; what most defined a person was his or her ability to participate in community. Rawls's understanding of the Protestant term "election" thus implied not removal from earthly fellowship but more profound relation to it. One "has not been elected for his own sake," he wrote, "but for the sake of others," for one joined "a communal process moving toward a communal end" of universal salvation.[9]

Given his obviously deep interest in religion as well as philosophy, Rawls next considered attending the Virginia Theological Seminary to study for the Episcopal priesthood. The pressures of World War II intervened, however; after graduating summa cum laude in philosophy in 1943, he joined the army. After basic infantry training, Rawls completed a course in the Signal Corps and was sent to the Pacific theater. He remained in service for three years, a member of F Company of the 128th Infantry Regiment of the 32nd Division, based primarily in New Guinea.

Rawls fought in the Philippines, at the bitter battles of Leyte and Luzon, and received a Bronze Star for his communication work behind enemy lines. He was grazed by a sniper's bullet but fortunately avoided more serious injury. He worked his way to the rank of sergeant but was demoted to private after refusing an officer's command, which he felt inappropriate, to discipline another soldier who had insulted the lieutenant. He left the service at that rank but not before serving four months in occupied Japan shortly after the United States dropped its two atomic bombs. Rawls's troop's train went right through the destroyed city of Hiroshima, and he never forgot the devastation. He never believed that the decision to use atomic weapons was justified, no matter what President Harry Truman said about how it had shortened the war and saved more lives than were lost.

After he returned from service early in 1946, Rawls turned away from Christianity, in good measure because of what he had seen in wartime. His experience tells a story familiar in midcentury America: in the wake of the atrocities of the war, many doubted that their Christian faith provided answers and direction. Much later, when Rawls sought to explain how and why he had left behind the faith in which he was raised, he recalled three telling incidents.

One had occurred during the battle for Leyte, where the U.S. troops had managed after much bloodshed to hold their position. A Lutheran priest preached a sermon after the battle in which he said, "God aimed our bullets at the Japanese while God protected us from theirs." This angered Rawls, who upbraided the minister "for saying what I assumed he knew perfectly well . . . [that these] were simply falsehoods about divine providence."[10] Rawls understood that the clergymen had said this to calm the troops but felt he ought not to have twisted Christian doctrine to do so.

The second incident occurred on the island of Luzon. Rawls had developed a close friendship with one of his fellow infantrymen. One day a sergeant came looking for two volunteers, one to go to scout Japanese positions, the other to give blood to a badly wounded soldier in a field hospital. The choice would be made on the basis of who had the right blood type for a match. Rawls had, and he got to stay behind. While the other soldier and an officer were scouting, the Japanese unleashed a mortar barrage, killing both men. Thinking back to his brothers' deaths, Rawls never forgot the randomness of his survival and deeply mourned the loss of a friend.

Like many Americans, Rawls learned about the Holocaust from a movie made by the soldiers who liberated the death camps, shown by the army information services. He was shaken to his core and began to question whether prayer was efficacious or necessary in the face of such barbarity. "How could I pray and ask God to help me or my family, or my country, or any other cherished thing I cared about," he asked, "when God would not save millions of Jews from Hitler?" When Abraham Lincoln had chosen to see the Civil War as God's punishment for the Southerners' sin of slavery, "deserved equally by the North and South," he had provided a way for all Americans to believe that despite the harrowing carnage, God acted "justly." But one could not understand the Holocaust in the same way. "To interpret history as expressing God's will," Rawls concluded, God's will "must accord with the most basic ideas of justice as we know them." For what else could "basic justice" be? Thus, he rejected "the idea of the supremacy of the divine will as hideous and evil."

In the following months and years, he rejected "more and more of the main doctrines of Christianity, and it became more and more alien to [him]."[11] Upon his discharge from the army, he became convinced that the questions begging answers—why his brother Bobby died while he had lived, why more people lived lives of excess while others could barely put food on the table, and what moral universe could account for the unspeakable horrors of World War II—had no explanations in the faith in which he had been raised.

Benefiting from the G.I. Bill, Rawls began graduate work in philosophy at Princeton. He spent three semesters there and another at Cornell, where Malcolm was now teaching, and then returned to Princeton to write his dissertation under Stace. His dissertation, "A Study on the Grounds of Ethical Knowledge: Considered with Reference to Judgments on the Moral Worth of Character," investigated how choice applied to ethical questions. At Cornell he had been influenced by the logician Max Black, who had studied with Wittgenstein and defended inductive reasoning as a way to establish proper moral concepts. They could be ascertained, Rawls came to believe, by careful observation of human nature.[12] Soon enough, he would come to see that a proper understanding of morality had to be based on universal standards that all willingly accepted, not on something as debatable and divisive, say, as Christian ethics.

Rawls remained at Princeton on a fellowship year after graduating and took courses in political thought and constitutional law, as well as in economics. In June 1949 he married Margaret Warfield Fox, who had studied art history at Pembroke (Brown), whom he had met a year earlier. The couple soon returned to Princeton, where from 1950 to 1952, under the blight of the McCarthy hearings, Rawls taught courses in philosophy.

He spent the following year on a Fulbright fellowship at Christ Church, Oxford, where he met several philosophers who influenced him greatly: H. L. A. Hart, J. L. Austin, Gilbert Ryle, Isaiah Berlin, and Stuart Hampshire, several of whom were working within Wittgenstein's tradition. In particular, influenced by Stephen Toulmin's adoption of his mentor Wittgenstein's notion that generally accepted rules governed human activity, Rawls soon began to consider ethical reasoning as a socially constituted practice whose rules an ethical philosopher might ascertain. The ethicist's goal, Toulmin argued, should be to bring peoples' conflicting aims and desires into a compatible system.[13] Everyone must follow the rules for everyone's benefit, he thought, or the practice would be unsatisfying and divisive. In ethical terms, this meant society should be a cooperative venture based in mutual advantage.

During this formative period another major influence on Rawls was game theory, particularly as set forth in John von Neumann and Oskar Morgenstern's *Theory of Games and Economic Behavior*, which he had discovered in a reading group at Princeton in the early 1950s.[14] Their book offered a new way to study economic behavior, from the perspective of strategic games. Economic agents have their own set of preferences, they argued, and know as well those of others playing in the elaborate "game" of economics. Just as each actor tries to maximize his own advantage and satisfaction, the analyst has to find some state of equilibrium in which he can assess the actions of all the opposed players. What if, thought Rawls, one could apply this same reasoning to the "game" of ethics, to elucidate the principles behind peoples' understanding of justice? Where might such a thought experiment lead?

After his return from England, Rawls accepted an assistant professorship at Cornell, joining his old teacher Malcolm and his former classmates Rogers Albritton and David Sachs, and served as one of the editors of the well-regarded *Philosophical Review*. By 1959, with four children, having published several important essays, he took a one-year visiting appointment at Harvard, which led to a full professorship at neighboring MIT.

MIT charged Rawls and linguist Noam Chomsky with building up the philosophy component of its humanities program, and soon enough Hilary Putnam (W. V. O. Quine's student) and James Thomson (visiting for a year from Oxford) joined the team. Rawls remained at MIT until 1962, when tiring of administrative duties in the humanities division, he accepted the offer of the Harvard Department of Philosophy to join them. The university had acted wisely, for Rawls was poised to revive the field of moral philosophy.

Toward *A Theory of Justice*

Incidents Rawls remembered most sharply from his childhood signal some of the concerns he carried with him into his philosophy classrooms. The loss of his two brothers to illness and of his friend in the war made the question of contingency—what Charles Sanders Peirce had termed "tychism," the role of chance—central to his thinking. So, too, his memories of segregated Baltimore and the class difference among summer people and permanent residents in Maine brought forward matters of race and class and their relation to inequality. Now, at Harvard, he confronted the question of the justness of the war in Vietnam, the fairness of the U.S. Selective Service's draft criteria, particularly the college student deferment, and President Lyndon Johnson's support for extended civil rights, the War on Poverty, and the realization of the "Great Society."

To Rawls, the kinds of problems that modern culture faced—be they concerning atomic warfare or the war on poverty—demanded institutional rather than individual responses. He approached the same problems of responsibility and obligation from the opposite end of the trench from Edwards and Emerson, for the challenges were no longer personal, and God was of no help. Only the older James, with his growing understanding of the twentieth-century's pluralism and his counsel of focused action at all costs, met him somewhere in the middle.

Rawls had a simple answer as to why the country justified going to war in Vietnam and persisted in waging it so viciously. The unequal distribution of property and wealth gave certain parties inordinate power to influence politics. Wealthy corporations backed certain candidates for office who then championed their benefactors' special interests, such as arms manufacture or production of the poisonous defoliant Agent Orange, who stood to benefit from a state of war. As to what lengths an individual could go to oppose the government's unjust actions, Rawls argued that the nation had to accept the minority's rights of conscience as they attempted to influence others. In democratic culture, conscientious objection was a citizen's right and could not be discouraged or repressed.

These and other ideas had occupied Rawls virtually from the completion of his dissertation at Princeton and found their way into the essays that he published in the 1960s. A year spent at the Center for Advanced Study at Stanford allowed him to work full-time on a manuscript in which he systematically examined the establishment and maintenance of justice in social institutions, a project distinct from one that treats the ethical obligation of individuals. In the twentieth century, what could one do about such problems as large-scale unemployment, inequalities in wealth and property, or abuses of human rights? What kind of society should a nation strive to build, he asked, to make justice as fairness the ultimate goal?

While Rawls acknowledged that individuals participate every day in any number of situations that demand justice, he was not interested in personal responses to specific situations. Rather, he sought to define it so that any individual could agree to its definition and implications, regardless of his or her special interests. The result would be an institutional order in which all had a guarantee of certain baseline rights. Rawls was revising the notion of the social contract that had defined Western civilization ever since David Hume and Jean-Jacques Rousseau. By extending their work, he wanted to design (while not necessarily describing *how* it could be achieved) a realistic modern utopia, a polity governed by the concept of fairness. But as he tackled the problem of a just society, he also recurred to his deep interest in Christian ethics and particularly his sense of salvation through community.

Rawls had a complex and vexed relationship to the philosophy of utilitarianism, theorized in its classic form in the works of Jeremy Bentham, John Stuart Mill, and Henry Sidgwick. By the time he began drafting *A Theory of Justice* in the 1960s, he realized that if he was to conceptualize a more convincing theory, he needed a different starting point, which proved to be that of social contract. Utilitarianism's guiding principle is that a morally proper action is that which produces the most good, rationally and impartially considered, for the greatest number of people. In this philosophy, *consequences* are always central. The state can thus curtail or sacrifice the rights of some individuals if warranted by the larger social good. Utilitarianism does not recognize equal moral worth, or as Rawls put it, does not take seriously distinctions between persons.[15]

But in a multicultural, pluralistic world, such distinctions were unavoidable. "Each person," he wrote, "has an inviolability founded on justice that even the welfare of society as a whole cannot override." In such a society, "the liberties of equal citizenship" had to be taken as settled, and the rights secured by justice not be subject to political bargaining or to the calculus of interests.[16] How people treat each other does not pertain to how they achieve some end but *is* the end itself. Ethics is the analysis of relations between people, not of any individual's highest good.

Rawls believed that moral people are both reasonable and rational. "Reasonable" implies they can understand and act from principles that specify fair terms of social cooperation—they have a sense of *justice*. "Rational" means that they can form, revise, and intelligently pursue a conception of personal welfare, both in the present and going forward—they have a conception of the *good*. A moral person thus has a notion of his or her good but also understands the relationship between it and larger principles that undergird a just society, guaranteeing other peoples' "good." A just social system, Rawls concluded, defines the scope within which individuals must develop their aims and "provides a framework of rights and opportunities and the means of satisfaction within and by the use of which these ends may be equitably pursued."[17]

A liberal society thus has to allow for various conceptions of the good, depending on a person's religion, upbringing, geographical location, and other contingent factors. But to be viable, these conceptions have to accord with certain basic rights. Justice defined by society's "basic structure," its political constitution and chief economic and social institutions, thus trumps individual good. Citizens have to design, create, and adjust their own aims and behavior so that there is, in Rawls's signature phrase, "justice as fairness."[18]

Reverting to an earlier interest in game theory, Rawls viewed the basic structure of society as a practice, a closed system. No longer concerned with Christian ethics per se, he focused on justice in a self-contained national community, not in more local circumstances such as a town or in the totality of the global order. Within such a closed system, citizens had to establish a cooperative venture for mutual advantage. By the end of the 1960s, returning from Stanford to become chair of the Philosophy Department at Harvard, through a plethora of lectures and publications in scholarly journals, Rawls put together these and other ideas in his highly acclaimed first book, *A Theory of Justice.*[19]

"Justice as Fairness"

Justice, Rawls wrote on the first page of his book, "is the first virtue of social institutions, as truth is to systems of thought." Whatever else social institutions accomplish for the welfare of mankind, they must not sacrifice justice. If a society chooses to help its people by creating better housing, for example, that is fine, as long as, in so doing, the effort in no way harms any person and thus maintains justice for all. For this reason, Rawls adds, "justice denies that the loss of freedom for some is made right by a greater good shared by others."[20] It is impermissible ever to sacrifice any individual's basic liberties for someone else's, or even for the whole society's, gain.

Rawls next points out that, as people organize in society, each wants to pursue his or her particular goals to improve one's situation. But because a varied population has varying conceptions of such goals and how they can be obtained, conflicts are bound to occur. A society therefore has to craft institutions to guarantee that whatever conflict arises can be resolved fairly. There has to be some way to choose among the various social arrangements to determine such differing advantages and to underwrite an agreement on the proper way to distribute shares of those goals. This led Rawls to conclude that certain principles of social justice had to undergird stable society. But how did one arrive at these principles?

Members of a society have to arrange its foundations by mutual consent. Reasonable people have to agree that major social institutions are responsible for the distribution of fundamental rights and duties, and for determining the division of advantages that would arise from social cooperation. The arrangement of this "basic structure"—the political, economic, and social warp of any society—guarantees its stability even as it allows for the consideration of individual ends. Any conflicts that subsequently arise should be resolved by the further application of the principles of the basic structure.

So, how do people arrive at such a social contract? Here, Rawls famously posited his "purely hypothetical agreement" created from an "original position of equality." To accomplish this, all must assume that no one individual knows his place in society, his class position, or his social status; nor does anyone know "his fortune in the distribution of natural assets and abilities, his intelligence, strength, and the like." Indeed, contracting parties do not even know their own particular conceptions of the good or their "special psychological propensities." Thus, the basic principles of justice are chosen, Rawls argued, in a felicitous phrase, by mutual consent "behind a veil of ignorance," the chief rule of the game being played and that to which all players have to consent.[21] By making it impossible for one segment of society to structure principles to favor themselves rather than others, this initial situation is fair because moral persons—that is, as rational beings with a sense of justice, not self-serving individuals eager to secure their own well-being—agree on it.

Unlike people who pursue differing interests to accord with their personal beliefs, here one assumes mutual *disinterest*. Behind the veil of ignorance, the consenting parties cannot assume any private conception of the good. They have to select their principles of social organization on the basis of their implications for *everyone*.

Rawls argues that, under such a circumstance, rational people will agree on two overarching moral principles. First, that there should be equality in the assignment of basic rights and duties. Second, that social and economic inequalities are only just if they result in compensating benefits for everyone, and in particular for the least advantaged members of society. The chief intuitive idea here is that any division of advantages should be such as to elicit the willing cooperation of everyone, including those less well situated. In this way, society modifies its original position only when it is for everyone's well-being.

Rawls assumed that these two principles could guide people through any unanticipated conflicts that arise as society evolves. For example, people know that religious intolerance and racial discrimination are unjust. All rational actors will agree to this principle, making such a conviction one of several provisional fixed points that any reasonable conception of justice must contain. But we have much less assurance about, say, the correct distribution of wealth or the disposition of authority. Confronted with this sort of problem, society either has to revise the original position or alter the conditions of the new, unanticipated situation to accord with that position. When a society arrives at consistency between its considered judgments about justice and any challenges to it, Rawls claims that it has reached a point of "reflective equilibrium."[22] People must strive to modify the original position to move toward such balance.

Next, Rawls elaborates two chief principles of justice that he believed were beyond debate. First, regarding society's political arrangement, he posits that each person must have an equal right to the most extensive scheme of equal basic liberties as long as it is compatible with a similar scheme for others. For example, a Christian cannot expect protection of one's right to worship and deny the same to a

Muslim, nor can an atheist persecute a Hindu. Second, economic and social inequalities are to be arranged so that they are "both (a) reasonably expected to be to everyone's advantage, and (b) attached to positions and offices open to all." This results in an egalitarianism that guarantees the proper distribution of the shares of "social primary goods"—that is, of rights, liberties, opportunities for personal betterment, income, and wealth.[23]

Inequalities, under the first principle, can never work to everyone's advantage. But the devil lies in the details of the second principle, for in attempting to structure the basic position in accordance with egalitarianism, conflicts among different parties are bound to occur. If certain structural inequalities are permissible, how are they to be distributed in procedures "open to all"? Does "careers open to talents" only mean "formal equality of opportunity in that all have at least the same legal rights of access to privileged positions"?[24] Or, given the discrimination that might be masked beneath such phrasing, should the positions be open not only in a formal sense but in such a way that all truly have a fair chance to obtain them? Conceived during the days of the War on Poverty and the Voting Rights Act of 1965, these and other questions were central to the "game" that an ethicist played.

True equality of opportunity implies not only that throughout society there are roughly equal prospects of achievement and personal fulfillment for everyone similarly motivated and endowed but also that social class or other such contingencies should not affect the expectations of those of the same abilities and aspirations. Hence, Rawls's opposition to the 2-s deferment in the draft, on the basis of the contingency of parents' differing incomes. In some cases, society has to redress such inequalities. "Those who have been favored by nature," he wrote, "may gain from their good fortune only on terms that improve the situation of those who have lost out."[25] It is true that the more advantaged are entitled to whatever they can acquire in accordance with the rules of a fair system of social cooperation. But given such subtleties, the problem is how to devise a basic structure of society to maintain justice for all.

Rawls turned to defining more carefully what he meant by his original position, refining the proposition that one has to construct society so as to allow its members to work toward "reflective equilibrium" as new challenges arise. People have different conceptions of the good, which lead them to different ends and purposes and to make conflicting claims on the natural and social resources available to them. A diversity of philosophical and religious beliefs, and of political and social doctrines, that have to be respected further color and partially determine such personal goals. When such new challenges arise, society must alter the original position by strictly deductive reasoning from the position's cardinal assumptions.

If a society is to maintain reflective equilibrium, again the principles agreed upon have to be universal in the sense that everyone accepts them. Once a society decides on such principles, arguments in support of certain claims cannot be adjudicated by any higher standard. Citizens must accept the reasoning from these principles as conclusive. The results of any deliberation based on them must override both the demands of law and custom, and of social rules generally, as well as any considerations of prudence or self-interest. Further, it is crucial that in such situations, parties understand that they have no basis for bargaining in the usual sense and cannot enter into agreements that they know they cannot keep. Rawls concludes that free, rational individuals, intent on creating a just society, will choose to order their community around a workable theory of social justice. His is a vision of community in which morality is defined not by the state or the pursuit of any higher good but by interpersonal relations.

Institutions

In the second part of his book, having settled on basic principles, Rawls addresses more deliberately the shape of institutions that guarantee such justice. When particular circumstances arise that test it, when there are conflicting opinions of it, what political mechanisms must be in place to reconcile such challenges? Rawls proposes a four-stage sequence.

The first stage is to establish the original position. The second is a "constitutional stage," in which people decide on political forms and adopt a constitution to institutionalize them, subject to the constraints of the principles of justice. In other words, people have to design a system to regulate the constitutional powers of government and protect the basic rights of citizens. Next comes a "legislative stage," when the veil of ignorance is lifted somewhat to allow reasoned consideration of the full range of economic and social facts that define the society.[26] Rawls understood that conflicts in the second stage are commonly subject to reasonable differences of opinion. In the legislative stage, they establish procedures to address those varied situations and opinions. Finally, the people have to consider how judges and administrators should apply rules to particular cases. In such cases, the veil of ignorance is totally removed, so that all parties have access to all pertinent information to resolve conflicts. Because all parties have ratified the society's basic principles, its overarching constitution, and its particular laws and policies, they are now in a position to live justly.

Rawls also addresses what civil and political liberties the state should ensure. First, there is liberty of conscience, a right guaranteed in the original position. But there must be limits to this, again based on the doctrine of equal rights for all. The government, for example, has the right to limit such liberty when it has to carry out its duty of impartially supporting the conditions necessary for peoples' pursuit of their own interests, as long as they do not threaten the common good.

But what is to be done if a citizen persists in intolerance of another's ideas? Rawls is clear. Society should restrict those who are intolerant "only when the tolerant sincerely and within reason believe that their own security and that of the institutions of liberty are in danger."[27] Otherwise, the intolerant must be tolerated. In such cases, people recognize that their differences are profound and cannot be reconciled through reason.

Rawls similarly dissects society's protection of political liberties. All citizens are guaranteed an equal right to take part in, and determine the outcome of, the constitutional process that establishes the laws with which they comply. More specifically, the constitution guarantees a representative government, regular elections, and firm constitutional protections for certain liberties, particularly freedom of speech and assembly, and liberty to form political associations. A problem in guaranteeing these rights, however, arises with regard to access to political office, for in this arena Rawls recognizes the outsize advantage that wealth conveys.

This is particularly true in the United States, where, historically, one of the main defects of its constitutional government has been a failure to ensure the fair value of political liberty. The American government, Rawls believed, has never seriously addressed campaign reform, for it is obvious that the nation's legal system tolerates disparities in the distribution of property and wealth that far exceeds what is compatible with political equality. When private contributions and not public funds finance parties and elections, the wishes of the dominant interest so constrain and determine the political forum that attempts to establish just constitutional rule are seldom properly addressed. The solution, however, sometimes sorely tests the system, particularly if there arises the thorny problem of the redistribution of wealth, a matter about which there can be considerable disagreement.

And what of other disparities that arise from the nature of economic institutions? The social system of which economic institutions compose a large part shapes the needs and aspirations of its citizens. But the economic system is not only an institutional device for satisfying existing needs but also of creating and fashioning these in the future. Because markets affect individual liberties and aspirations, providing a basic level of wealth to all citizens may be necessary. A just society has to provide for those at the lower rungs of society, what Rawls calls the guarantee of a "social minimum."[28]

Finally, he examines a citizen's obligations under such a government. All citizens have a duty to support and further just institutions, which implies two things. First, people have to comply with and do their share to support the institutions, for that is the only way to establish just community. Second, they must work toward the establishment of just arrangements when they do not yet exist, at least when this can be done with little cost to themselves. Lastly, citizens must accept the duty of mutual aid to those in immediate need.

But what of the obligation to obey society's laws that one feels are unjust?[29] When the basic structure of society is reasonably just, he writes, citizens must recognize unjust laws as binding, provided that they do not exceed certain limits of injustice. They must do this because they have consented to the system that established such laws. As difficult as this might be to accept, citizens have to believe in political process and judicial review. When someone objects to what one considers an unjust law, Rawls continued, its resolution is not a compromise, "a bargain struck between opposing parties trying to advance their ends." Rather, there has to be an attempt to find the best policy for all as defined by the agreed upon principles of justice. If the political process works as it should, the exchange of opinions with others checks partiality and widens perspective. As the limits of their vision are brought home, disputing parties should strive to see things from another standpoint. This is what Rawls called "deliberative democracy."[30]

In the third part of his book Rawls considers how, once people establish a "well-ordered society" in which everyone accepts and knows that the others accept the same principles of justice, and whose basic social situations satisfy these principles, people will acquire and maintain a sense of justice.

He first considers self-respect, perhaps the most important primary good. It is a person's sense of his own value, "his secure conviction that his conception of the good, his plan of life, is worth carrying out," as well as a confidence in his ability, so far as it is within his power, to fulfill his intentions. A society supports the essential good of self-respect, he claims, when it encourages and enables one to have a rational plan of life that makes one feel that life is worth living and when one finds oneself and one's deeds "appreciated and confirmed by others who are likewise esteemed and their association enjoyed."[31] This characterizes good citizenship.

A person who does not have such support, Rawls claims, feels a sense of shame. Not regret, "the general feeling aroused by the loss or absence of what we think good for us," but a powerful negative emotion evoked by shocks to a person's self-respect. To eliminate this debilitating condition there must be congruence between the "right," which all must affirm, and the "good," which can vary from individual to individual. When one considers what others define as the good, what they seek in life, one's opinions must only be advisory, unlike when one speaks of the "right," to which every individual must be committed by acceptance of the principles of justice.[32]

Rawls also explores the problem of a society's stability, considering how over time a society maintains its citizens' allegiance to the original principles. One conception of justice, he maintains, is more stable than another if the sense of justice that it engenders is stronger and more likely to override disruptive inclinations and if the institutions it allows foster weaker and fewer impulses and temptations to act unjustly. In this sense, stability does not mean that an institution cannot change or evolve as new demands arise but rather that society's organization must be sufficiently malleable to allow such readjustment. Once people realize how social arrangements arising from principles of justice have promoted their good and that of those with whom they are affiliated, they will develop a desire to act on those principles. Here, stability is a function of how well society allows individual self-development.

There also must be "congruence" between a person's perception of the good and a sense of justice. In a well-ordered society, that is, does a person's rational plan of life support and affirm his or her sense of justice? Congruence means that when members of society consider their life plans, they choose to maintain justice as regulative of interpersonal relations. Then, there will be a strong bond between citizens, because the success of just institutions is the agreed upon end of all members of society.

Rawls would go on to write two more important works, *Political Liberalism* (1993) and *The Law of Peoples* (1999). In the first, he addressed the fact that in modern democracies all citizens are incapable of affirming the same doctrine. Without any shared religious, moral, or philosophical ideals, what forms the basis for a shared conception of citizenship? However vehemently factions, defined by denomination, political party, or class affiliation, could feud during Edwards's, Emerson's, or even James's lifetimes, the overwhelming common agreement was that a monotheistic God sat in some degree of benevolent judgment over humankind and their actions. Whatever one's standing in society, the final accounting would occur before the Lord.

It wasn't just that Rawls appreciated that states confronted a plurality of interests, making some such citizens' principles simply incompatible. He realized that in pluralistic societies the principle of justice as fairness can never be satisfactorily stabilized. Rawls tackled the project of establishing how, for the "right reasons," one might develop "a political conception of political justice" for a "constitutional democratic" society whose citizens adhered to a plurality of reasonable doctrines, religious and nonreligious, liberal and nonliberal.[33]

Rawls's solution was a new liberal democratic theory of citizenship. In a pluralistic society, he wrote, free and equal citizens cannot expect all others to share their goals, but they should be able to respect one another's interests. He was aware that the key question is whether such a society can remain stable as its citizens encounter challenges to that mutual respect. Again, he posits a freestanding principle of justness as fairness, presented apart from any other comprehensive doctrine, so that it is not owned in greater or lesser degree by any particular citizens. It is something, in other words, to which one can agree regardless of one's other beliefs. If citizens can agree to such a freestanding principle on which to base "public reasoning," they can elaborate and share a political discourse that flows from the principle of justice essential to the structure of society.[34]

If they exercise such reasoning, they possess a sense of justice that leads them to pursue rationally a conception of the good in ways that respect pluralism. This forms the basis for citizenship in a liberal, democratic society. No matter what moral, philosophical, ideological, or religious doctrines citizens hold, they seek to pursue the same "primary goods," that is, the same basic rights and liberties, economic opportunities, and the right to election to positions of authority and responsibility, all undergirded by the promise of mutual self-respect. These goals are mediated and maintained by public reason, "the guidelines of public inquiry" between citizens, that Rawls believes must accompany any compelling conception of political justice.[35] To be free and public, such debate demands a democratic politics. Because citizens agree that they will not reach agreement on all issues, they pledge to resort to public reason to resolve any conflicts that arise.

After Rawls had formulated his principles of democratic equality for a pluralistic society, he had one more step to take. Thus far he had theorized that the societies in question were closed and self-contained individual entities—nation states, really—separate from other societies. But how should one extend his theorization to the realm of international law and justice? In his third book, *The Law of Peoples* (1999), he addresses the question of whether the creation of an "international Society of liberal and decent *Peoples*" might be possible.[36] As had been his method in the domestic cases, he focused on the institutional structures that would be necessary for agreement on international standards that accorded with justice as fairness.

Rawls does not regard these rights as ethnocentric: they are *universal* human rights that do not depend on any comprehensive religious, philosophical, or political doctrine. Respect for them marks membership in the Society of Peoples. Even in such a society in which there may not be equal representation, each person is recognized as a cooperating member of the group and, in any political decisions, all groups within the hierarchy are consulted.

The Law of Peoples thus argues for the encouragement of a relatively just and well-ordered international order and acknowledges the universality of basic human rights. With this book, Rawls completed his magisterial treatment of the meaning and establishment of justice among citizens and peoples. It was an exploratory and explanatory project to settle the question of how one creates and maintains a just and fair society and how those same principles can be employed to bring greater justice to the world.

Injustice and Inequality

It is important briefly to address the sharpest rebuttals to Rawls's work, those of his Harvard colleagues Robert Nozick and political scientist Michael J. Sandel. In *Anarchy, State, Utopia* (1974), Nozick criticized Rawls from a libertarian position, that is, as someone who values individual rights and freedom over any sort of coercion or even direction—including distributive justice—from the state.[37] Nozick does not accept Rawls's notions of the original position and veil of ignorance. Instead, he emphasizes that each individual has basic rights, liberties, and opportunities—dependent on the vagaries of history, social circumstances, and natural endowments—that cannot be set aside, as Rawls wants them to be when citizens establish the original position. Nozick objects to Rawls's scheme because it eventuates in an interventionist government that might ride roughshod over property rights and abrogate certain agreements between private parties, all for the goal of distributive justice.

Instead of Rawls's egalitarian vision, Nozick posits what he calls an "entitlement theory of justice" more amenable to individual rights and liberties (particularly property rights), and that can be characterized as very laissez-faire. Any welfare-state schema that includes distributive justice, Nozick believes, eventually impinges on freedom. Rawls sought a principle of equality with respect to peoples' *needs*, while Nozick wants a principle of equality with respect to *entitlements*. To him, an egalitarian theory of justice is problematic because of its potential interference in an individual's basic rights. His entitlement theory relies on historical principles that recognize past circumstances or actions of people can create different entitlements or different deserts to things.

Rawls's system restricts our rights and Nozick's preserves our liberties; but one can only decide which system is more just *after* a people decide what their rights and liberties are, something that they have to establish from the "original position." Only then can one decide which principles should determine the acquisition and transfer of goods. Once that schema is in place, Rawls argues, procedural justice will determine whatever reallocation of goods is necessary. The design of the rules in the original position thus is the key to distributive justice. As a people think through the original position, they assess and structure a society's distributional needs. After that, procedural rules determine the proper distribution of goods. It is not that government interferes with the just transfer of or unfairly redistributes goods but carefully formulates the rules for such redistribution *when the society is formed*, and the original position agreed upon. Rawls concludes we have a right to our natural abilities and a right to whatever we become entitled to by taking part in a fair social process. The problem that he addressed (and that Nozick avoided) is to characterize that process, to embody justice as fairness as completely as possible.

Nozick was also concerned that, in Rawls's scheme, every member of society might not receive the full value of one's contribution to it. Those who are untalented, for example, get something that is good for them, while the talented have to accept that, even if they can do better on their own, they have to agree with whatever redistribution justice demands. If the share of the talented is smaller than what they can produce on their own, Nozick argued, they have the right to refuse cooperation, because they gain nothing tangible by it and lose some of what might have come of their contributions to society. There is no reason for them to cooperate if under such a social contract their goods are somehow diminished.

Rawls, on the other hand, invokes the "difference" principle. This is an agreement to regard the distribution of natural talents as in some respects a "common," "social," or "collective" asset. Society should benefit from the distribution and diversity of talents among its members: all become better because of the varied gifts each brings to society. He understands that the distribution of talents is arbitrary and thus, in a sense, undeserved, given as they are at birth. Yes, a person has a right to use and profit from his or her talents. These cannot be hijacked or requisitioned—in slavery, say—without consent. And talents certainly can be rewarded according to the good they do. But they are morally inconsequential, having nothing to do with a person's character. Thus, they should be structured so that the common good is advanced, even among the untalented.

Rawls's other Harvard colleague, Sandel, took issue with his ideas from a different direction, a *communitarian* position. In *Liberalism and the Limits of Justice* (1982), he argued that Rawls underestimated the importance of an individual's membership in a community.[38] To achieve an original position, Rawls's subjects have to abandon what in fact defines them—their goals, ambitions, memberships, friendships, and other constitutive commitments. They have to do this because such attachments necessarily color what they considered just; they would act in too self-reflexive a way. To be clear, after establishing the original position, people are free to form whatever attachments they wish, as long as justice still reigns. Sandel, however, insists that the notion of an unencumbered self simply is unrealistic. The goal of a just institution does not provide the kind of glue necessary to hold together disparate individuals.

Sandel also claimed that, rather than trying to institute justice over morally deficient individuals, we should try to eliminate those things among us that cause disagreements. Justice finds its occasion, he believed, because people cannot know each other, or each other's ends, well enough to govern by the common good alone. This condition is not likely to be eliminated, and as long as it is not, a sense of justice will be necessary. Rawls argues, rather, that there will always be diversity among peoples and that this should be celebrated. But because diversity is always present and arises through peoples' having made reasonable choices to follow particular paths, there is need for a conception of justice to control interpersonal relations. People cannot, as Sandel envisions, return to some prelapsarian past before conflicts arose and in which they all are members of the same community.

Instead, Rawls envisions a reasonable pluralism. The single unified community that Sandel posits is no longer a political possibility for those who accept the constraints of liberty and toleration of democratic institutions.

Suffice it to say that first Rawls and later his acolytes have ably answered these and other criticisms, like those of Michael Walzer, for example, whose *Spheres of Justice* (1983) offered yet another communitarian critique, specifically that Rawls was not sensitive enough to how different kinds of societies might affirm different values. As Walzer puts it, "Justice is relative to social meanings."[39] Here it is important to consider the implications of Rawls's work for American domestic policy that lay just beneath the surface of many of his chief arguments.

His main purpose in *A Theory of Justice*, for example, was to explore the obligations that justify the creation of a state and the extent to which it can compel individuals to act for the benefit the whole, while still preserving each person's dignity. He understood that his theory did not apply to all peoples but only to those in "a democratic society under modern conditions," that is a Western nation like the United States. His goal was a polity that practices justness as fairness. A glance at the contemporary situation in the United States, however, divided as it was in the 1960s over civil rights, the War on Poverty, and military intervention abroad, undeniably proved that the nation had failed to realize such a polity. Rawls tried to develop a moral philosophy that would help right the ship of state.

Hence, his book was implicitly a compelling defense of the welfare state. Over time, the U.S. Constitution, which provided the country's initial blueprint, has increasingly seemed inadequate to the complexities of a pluralistic, multicultural democracy. Inequalities of wealth and restrictions of civil and human rights—in slavery, in segregated schools, in delimited immigration, in prisons, and at the ballot box, to give just a few examples—demanded new ways to make citizens feel responsible for the consideration and care of all segments of society.

In staking out his position, Rawls reignited an internal debate that the country had conducted virtually from its initial settlement by Europeans. To Rawls, the commonwealth mattered more than the individual, as long as no individuals were forced from their honestly acquired positions or deprived of their basic liberties. The debate between Harvard's leading philosophers was over the relationship between the individual and the state, which for centuries had been arbitrated by a Christian God. Rawls sought nothing less than to reconfigure the terms of that relationship for a post-Christian world.

Coda

From the seventeenth century to the present, the colonies, and later the United States, have periodically debated how to achieve what Abraham Lincoln called "a more perfect union," something that many people think is best described, in the United States, in the Constitution and Bill of Rights. But the work to which Lincoln urged Americans remains unfinished. Was the initial establishment of this New Jerusalem across the Atlantic for the guarantee and celebration of individual sovereignty? Or was it to establish a more inclusive community, a place where no one would ever leave another behind? Whether in 1740, 1836, 1900, 1971, or 2021, many things—slavery, the American Indian removal, the transportation and communication revolutions, the abolition movement, social Darwinism, the attempt to regulate monopolies, the contest for civil rights, campaigns to end poverty, the Cold War, and now, immigration from war-torn countries—have challenged the Constitution, what we might term, in Rawls's words, the country's "original position."

Rawls knew that Americans still had to debate what, through reason and compromise, might make the nation realize and preserve the kinds of polity that the Puritans, the Founding Fathers, Edwards, Emerson, and James sought to define in their different ways. Too often Americans submit to the diminishment or cooptation of their intellectual history. Theirs is an unhelpful, perhaps pernicious, view that encourages the sort of myopic expressions that we find in Andrew Carnegie's oversimplification of Emerson's thought.

Ignorance of the ideas of such people as Edwards, Emerson, James, and Rawls devalues not just these but how other theorists of American democracy have contributed to the chief national dialogue. Such ignorance means that when we confront inevitable change or roadblocks or external and internal threats, we are less likely to reach for new ideas rather than for other, more easily accessible and perhaps more applicable tools. The worst outcome is the gradual, progressive attenuation of our history.

Rawls tried to bring back his readers into healthy and constructive dialogue with their past. Although in each generation the context of ideas changes, one principle remains the same: the nation's bedrock belief that every individual's life and values are worth as much as anyone else's. As separated temporally as were the four thinkers herein discussed, their ideas centered on how one might balance individual sovereignty and communal responsibility, a problem that has haunted the United States since European settlement in the seventeenth century when English Puritans left their homeland because of how corrupt (and, for many, how impoverished) it had become. As Robert Cushman, clergyman to the Pilgrim group in Plymouth put it just before they removed to the New World, "the straitness of the place [England] is such as each man is fain to pluck his means, as it were, out of his neighbor's throat." There is "such pressing and oppressing in town and country," he continued, "about farms, trades, traffic, etc., so a man can hardly any where set up a trade but he shall pull down two of his neighbors." The land, Cushman concluded, "groaneth under so many close-fisted and unmerciful men."[1] To people of Cushman's and other Puritans' persuasion, the lands across the Atlantic offered the chance for moral as well as spiritual reformation.

Cushman's powerful words call to mind two other works: John Winthrop's "Model of Christian Charity," delivered to another group of Puritans as they were about to cross the Atlantic in 1630; and as well, another urtext in American history, Thomas Jefferson's Declaration of Independence. Both have been cited by generations of politicians who have striven to remind us of, and recall us to, our country's purpose. The documents outline starkly opposed moral visions.

"We shall be as a city on a hill," Winthrop wrote, "the eyes of the world will be upon us," words that have proved fodder to those who claim America's exceptionalism, its special place in world affairs. But there is more. In this sermon Winthrop argues that all men and women are *not* created equal but have different callings and different gifts. "GOD ALMIGHTY in his most holy and wise providence, hath soe disposed of the condition of mankind, as in all times some must be rich, some poore, some high and eminent in power and dignitie; others mean and in submission." And why? So "that every man might have need of others, and from hence they might be all knitt more nearly together in the Bonds of brotherly affection."[2]

Puritan minister Thomas Hooker, in *The Danger of Desertion*, realized that this ethic no longer ruled in old England: "Learne therefore to heare and feare," he warned, "God can be a God without England." For even though God had been as "a mirror of mercy" to the country, God "may leave us," he wrote, "and make us a mirror of his justice."[3] To succeed as a colony, the Puritans needed what Winthrop counseled. Not to adhere to it would lead to the failure of their experiment. Winthrop, again:

> Now the onely way to avoyde this shipwracke, and to provide for our posterity, is to followe the counsell of Micah, *to doe justly, to love mercy, to walk humbly with our God.* For this end, wee must be knitt together, in this worke, as one man. Wee must entertaine each other in brotherly affection. Wee must be willing to abridge ourselves of our superfluities, for the supply of other's necessities. Wee must uphold a familiar commerce together in all meekeness, gentlenes, patience and liberality. Wee must delight in eache other; make other's conditions our oune; rejoice together, mourne together, labour and suffer together, allwayes haueving before our eyes our commission and community in the worke, as members of the same body.[4]

Now consider the country's other foundational document, in which Jefferson declared that all men are created equal and have an inalienable right to life, liberty, and the pursuit of happiness. While Winthrop counsels the need for love and cooperation, Jefferson codifies the sacred rights of the individual, the foundation of the modern liberal state, in which self is set off from society and, I would argue, by implication, from the commonwealth. Winthrop places Americans on a starting line and urges them to run toward the goal of social harmony, while Jefferson's aim is the kind of self-sufficiency and economic competence that Benjamin Franklin championed.

But while Winthrop's Puritans join hands and move toward that goal together, the strong helping the weak, Jefferson's Americans—white men who held a certain amount of property—all begin to run but do not hold hands. Some lose their way, others proceed more slowly, and only some cross the finish line, still viewing from afar their purported goal of social harmony. Emerson's friend Henry David Thoreau wryly described the result. "Men have an indistinct notion," he wrote, "that if they keep up this activity of joint stocks and spades long enough, all will at length ride somewhere, in next to no time, and for nothing." But, he continued, "though a crowd rushes to the depot, and the conductor shouts 'All aboard!' when the smoke is blown away and the vapor condensed, it will be perceived that few are riding, but the rest are run over."[5]

These brief glimpses into the country's history typify the centuries-long debates about the relative merits of an incipient communitarianism and those that result in a more individualistic, libertarian society. At different times and in different situations, many Americans praised how Edwards, Emerson, James, and Rawls attempted to outline an equitable, democratic polity, one that might deliver both liberty and justice for all. These thinkers discussed how European settlers in the New World and, later, citizens of the United States of America, could achieve and maintain the delicate balance between self and society, and thus realize the destiny to which they believed Americans had been called. We do well to consider their lessons as each tried to weave the various strands of God, self, community, and state into the woof of the elaborate, still-unfinished tapestry that composes the nation's history.

Notes

Introduction

1. See *Some Thoughts on the Religious Revivals* (1742), in *The Works of Jonathan Edwards*, 26 vols. (New Haven, Conn.: Yale University Press, 1957–2008), 4:352.

2. See Alfred Owen Aldridge, "Jonathan Edwards and William Godwin on Virtue," *American Literature* 18, no. 4 (January 1947): 308–18; and William Godwin, *An Enquiry Concerning Political Justice and Its Influence on General Virtue and Happiness*, 2 vols. (London, 1793), 1:19.

3. *Benjamin Franklin's Autobiography*, ed. Joyce E. Chaplin (New York: W. W. Norton, 2012), 87.

4. Henry David Thoreau, "Resistance to Civil Government" (1849), in *Reform Papers* (Princeton, N.J.: Princeton University Press, 1973), 89.

5. Andrew Carnegie, "The Road to Business Success," in *The Empire of Business* (New York: Doubleday and Page, 1902), 18. He first delivered this lecture in Pittsburgh in 1885.

Chapter 1. Jonathan Edwards: Heaven Is a World of Love

1. The best biography of Chauncy is Edward M. Griffin, *Old Brick: Charles Chauncy of Boston, 1705–1787* (Minneapolis: University of Minnesota Press, 1980), from which most of this section is gleaned.

2. Good studies of the eighteenth-century revivals in British North America are Thomas S. Kidd, *The Great Awakening: The Roots of Evangelical Christianity in Colonial America* (New Haven, Conn.: Yale University Press, 2007); and Frank Lambert, *Inventing the "Great Awakening"* (Princeton, N.J.: Princeton University Press, 1999).

3. On Whitefield, see Frank Lambert, *"Pedlar in Divinity": George Whitefield and the Transatlantic Revivals, 1737–1770* (Princeton, N.J.:

Princeton University Press, 1991); Harry S. Stout, *Divine Dramatist: George Whitefield and the Rise of Modern Evangelicalism* (Grand Rapids, Mich.: W. B. Eerdmans, 1991); and, earlier, John Gillies, *Memoirs of Rev. George Whitefield* (Middletown, Conn.: Hunt and Noyes, 1838).

4. On Davenport's antics, see Harry S. Stout and Peter S. Onuf, "James Davenport and the Great Awakening in New London," *Journal of American History* 70 (December 1983): 556–78; and on the more radical New Lights in general, Douglas L. Winiarski, *Darkness Falls on the Land of Light: Experiencing Religious Awakenings in Eighteenth-Century New England* (Chapel Hill: University of North Carolina Press, 2017).

5. Charles Chauncy, "A Letter to the Rev. James Davenport . . . July 17, 1742," preface to Chauncy's *Enthusiasm Described and Caution'd Against* (Boston: J. Draper for S. Eliot and J. Blanchard, 1742).

6. Biographical details of Edwards's life are from Samuel Hopkins, *Life and Character of the Late Reverend Mr. Jonathan Edwards* (Boston: Kneeland, 1765), reprinted in David Levin, ed., *Jonathan Edwards: Profile* (New York: Hill and Wang, 1969); S. E. Dwight, *Life of President Edwards* (New York: G.& C.& H. Carvill, 1830); George Marsden, *Jonathan Edwards: A Life* (New Haven, Conn.: Yale University Press, 2003); and my *Jonathan Edwards: America's Evangelical* (New York: Hill and Wang, 2003).

7. "On Sarah Pierpont," in *The Works of Jonathan Edwards*, 26 vols. (New Haven, Conn.: Yale University Press, 1957–2008), 16:789–90.

8. Hopkins, *Life and Character*, 40–43; Dwight, *Life*, 107–10.

9. "A Divine and Supernatural Light," in Edwards, *Works*, 17:410–24.

10. See *A Faithful Narrative of the Surprising Work of God* (London, 1737), in Edwards, *Works*, 4:130–212.

11. "Letter to Colman," May 30, 1735, in Edwards, *Works*, 4:103.

12. Timothy Cutler to Zachary Grey, June 5, 1735, in John Nichols, *Illustrations of the Literary History of the Eighteenth Century*, 8 vols. (London: for the author, 1817–58), 4:298.

13. *Faithful Narrative*, in Edwards, *Works*, 4:158.

14. Chauncy, *Enthusiasm Described*, 3–5.

15. Charles Chauncy, *Seasonable Thoughts on the State of Religion* (Boston: J. Draper, 1742), 323–27; *Religious Affections*, in Edwards, *Works*, 2:120.

16. Chauncy, *Seasonable Thoughts*, 380.

17. *Some Thoughts on the Religious Revivals*, in Edwards, *Works*, 4:353.

18. *History of Redemption*, in Edwards, *Works*, 9:436. Also see C. C.

Goen, "Jonathan Edwards: A New Departure in Eschatology," *Church History* 28, no. 1 (March 1959): 25–40; and Nathan Friend, "Inventing Revivalist Millennialism: Edwards and the Scottish Connection," *Journal of Religious History* 42, no. 1 (March 2018), 52–71.

19. See David D. Hall, ed., *The Antinomian Controversy, 1636–1638: A Documentary History* (1968; repr., Durham, N.C.: Duke University Press, 1990); and Michael P. Winship, *Making Heretics: Militant Protestantism and Free Grace in Massachusetts, 1636–1641* (Princeton, N.J.: Princeton University Press, 2002).

20. Chauncy, *Seasonable Thoughts*, xxv–xxvi.

21. Ibid., 372n.

22. Edwards to William McCulloch, March 5, 1743, in Edwards, *Works*, 16:135–36.

23. "Heaven Is a World of Love," in Edwards, *Works*, 8:373.

24. Ibid., 8:392.

25. Ibid., 8:393, 396.

26. "A Copy of a Covenant," in Edwards, *Works*, 16:121–22.

27. On the state of Northampton's economy in this period, see Patricia J. Tracy, *Jonathan Edwards, Pastor: Religion and Society in Eighteenth-Century Northampton* (New York: Farrar, Straus, and Giroux, 1980), especially chap. 4.

28. "A Copy of a Covenant," in Edwards, *Works*, 16:122–23.

29. Edwards, *Works*, 4:146; Edwards to Thomas Gillespie, July 1, 1751, in Edwards, *Works*, 16:380–81.

30. Tracy, *Jonathan Edwards, Pastor*, 38–39.

31. Ibid., 38–42.

32. *Treatise Concerning Religious Affections*, in Edwards, *Works*, 2:97.

33. Ibid., 2:96–97.

34. Ibid., 2:99, 120.

35. Ibid., 2:197, 205–6.

36. Ibid., 2:260.

37. Ibid., 2:373.

38. Ibid., 2:379.

39. Ibid., 2:383.

40. "Narrative of the Communion Controversy," in Edwards, *Works*, 12:509.

41. This work is found in its entirety in volume 12 of Edwards, *Works*.

42. Hopkins, *Life and Character*, 54.

43. Edwards to Thomas Foxcroft, May 24, 1749, in Edwards, *Works*, 16:283–84; and Edwards to John Erskine, July 5, 1750, 16:355; Hopkins, *Life and Character*, 63.

44. *Freedom of the Will*, in Edwards, *Works*, 1:364.

45. *The End for Which God Created the World*, in Edwards, *Works*, 8:424.

46. Ibid., 8:531, 533.

47. Ibid., 8:535–36.

48. *The Nature of True Virtue*, in Edwards, *Works*, 8:540–41.

49. Ibid., 8:540–42.

50. Edwards to Trustees of the College of New Jersey, October 19, 1757, in Edwards, *Works*, 16:725–30.

51. See, for example, Henry F. May, *The Enlightenment in America* (New York: Oxford University Press, 1973), esp. 1–152; and Caroline Winterer, *American Enlightenments: Pursuing Happiness in the Age of Reason* (New Haven, Conn.: Yale University Press, 2016), 18–40 and 171–96.

52. Harriet Beecher Stowe, *Oldtown Folks* (Boston: Fields, Osgood, 1869), 395.

53. Biographical details come from Mark Valeri, *Law and Providence in Joseph Bellamy's New England: The Origins of the New Divinity in Revolutionary America* (New York: Oxford University Press, 1994); and Tryon Edwards's "Memoir" in the first volume of *The Works of Joseph Bellamy, D.D.*, 2 vols. (Boston: Congregational Board of Publication, 1850).

54. Joseph Bellamy, "Personal Account," in Valeri, *Law and Providence*, 16–17.

55. *Literary Diary of Ezra Stiles, D.D.*, ed. Franklin Bowditch Dexter, 3 vols. (New York: Scribner's, 1901), 3:385.

56. See John Corrigan, *The Hidden Balance: Religion and the Social Theories of Charles Chauncy and Jonathan Mayhew* (New York: Cambridge University Press, 1987).

57. *The Works of the Reverend Joseph Bellamy*, 3 vols. (New York: Dodge, 1811–12), 1:43.

58. Ibid., 1:78–79.

59. Ibid., 1:69–97.

60. *Literary Diary of Ezra Stiles*, 3:361.

61. Biographical details come from Joseph A. Conforti, *Samuel Hopkins and the New Divinity Movement* (Grand Rapids, Mich.: Wm. B. Eerdmans,

1981); Edwards Amasa Park's "Memoir" in the first volume of *The Works of Samuel Hopkins, D.D.*, 3 vols. (Boston: Congregational Board of Publication, 1854); and Stephen West, *Sketches of the Life of the Late Rev. Samuel Hopkins* (Hartford, Conn.: Hudson and Goodwin, 1805).

62. Park, "Memoir," *The Works of Samuel Hopkins*, 1:30–31.

63. Charles Chauncy, *The Benevolence of the Deity* (Boston: Powers and Willis, 1784), 11, 14.

64. David Ramsay, *The Life of George Washington* (New York: Hopkins and Seymour, 1809), 373, 331–32.

65. See David W. Kling, *A Field of Divine Wonders: The New Divinity and Village Revivals in Northwest Connecticut, 1792–1822* (University Park: Pennsylvania State University Press, 1993).

66. Harriet Beecher Stowe, *The Minister's Wooing* (New York: Derby and Jackson, 1859), 334; and "New England Ministers," *Atlantic Monthly* 1, no. 4 (February 1858): 476.

67. Reinhold Niebuhr, *The Irony of American History* (1952; repr., Chicago: University of Chicago Press, 2010), 63.

Chapter 2. Ralph Waldo Emerson: The Infinitude of the Common Man

1. See John Corrigan, *The Hidden Balance: Religion and the Social Theories of Charles Chauncy and Jonathan Mayhew* (New York: Cambridge University Press, 1987). For a biography, see Charles W. Akers, *Called unto Liberty: A Life of Jonathan Mayhew* (1964; repr., Cambridge: Harvard University Press, 2013).

2. The standard history of American Unitarianism's emergence is Conrad E. Wright, *The Beginnings of Unitarianism in America* (Boston: Starr King Press, 1955); but also see Daniel Walker Howe, *The Unitarian Conscience: Harvard Moral Philosophy, 1805–1861* (Cambridge: Harvard University Press, 1970).

3. See David W. Kling, *A Field of Divine Wonders: The New Divinity and Village Revivals in Northwest Connecticut, 1792–1822* (University Park: Pennsylvania State University Press, 1993).

4. See Jerry Wayne Brown, *The Rise of Biblical Criticism in America: The*

New England Scholars (Middletown, Conn.: Wesleyan University Press, 1969).

5. Edward Dorr Griffin to James Richards, January 15, 1810, in William Sprague, *Memoir of the Rev. Edward D. Griffin, D.D.* (New York: Taylor and Dodd, 1839), 116.

6. For a good account of Beecher's life see *The Autobiography of Lyman Beecher*, ed. Barbara M. Cross, 2 vols. (1864; repr., Cambridge: Harvard University Press, 1961). Also, Vincent Harding, *A Certain Magnificence: Lyman Beecher and the Transformation of American Protestantism, 1775–1868* (Brooklyn, N.Y.: Carlson, 1991) and Marie Caskey, *Chariot of Fire: Religion and the Beecher Family* (New Haven, Conn.: Yale University Press, 1977).

7. See Kenneth Silverman, *Timothy Dwight* (New York: Twayne, 1969).

8. *Autobiography of Lyman Beecher*, 2:48.

9. Ibid., 1:402, 2:35.

10. Lyman Beecher, "The Faith Once Delivered to the Saints," in the *Works of Lyman Beecher*, 3 vols. (Boston: John P. Jewett, 1852), 2:259.

11. Ibid., 2:48.

12. Lyman Beecher, "The Bible a Code of Laws," in *Works of Lyman Beecher*, 2:154.

13. Ibid., 2:83–84.

14. Ibid., 2:54–55.

15. Beecher to Catharine Beecher, November 1829, cited in *Autobiography of Lyman Beecher*, 2:167, 170. One of the lyrics was, "While Beecher's church holds out to burn / The vilest sinner may return."

16. Manuscript sermon, 1830, cited in Mary Kupiec Cayton, *Emerson's Emergence: Self and Society in the Transformation of New England, 1800–1845* (Chapel Hill: University of North Carolina Press, 1989), 108.

17. This biographical section depends on several fine biographies, viz., Robert D. Richardson Jr., *Emerson: The Mind on Fire* (Berkeley: University of California Press, 1995); Gay Wilson Allen, *Waldo Emerson* (New York: Viking, 1981); and John McAleer, *Ralph Waldo Emerson: Days of Encounter* (Boston: Little Brown, 1984). Also see Lawrence Buell, *Emerson* (Cambridge: Harvard University Press, 2003).

18. On Mary Moody Emerson, see Phyllis Cole, *Mary Moody Emerson and the Origins of Transcendentalism: A Family History* (New York: Oxford University Press, 1998).

19. Ibid., 132.

20. On Channing and his considerable influence on Emerson, see Andrew Delbanco, *William Ellery Channing: An Essay on the Liberal Spirit in America* (Cambridge: Harvard University Press, 1981).

21. Edith Emerson Gregg, ed., *Our First Love: The Letters of Ellen Tucker Emerson to Ralph Waldo Emerson* (Cambridge: Harvard University Press, 1962), 68.

22. Ralph Waldo Emerson, "The Lord's Supper," in *Essays and Lectures* (New York: Library of America, 1983), 137.

23. Ralph Waldo Emerson to Mary Moody Emerson, August 19, 1832, in *The Letters of Ralph Waldo Emerson*, ed. Ralph L. Rusk, 6 vols. (New York: Columbia University Press, 1939), 1:375.

24. See Brown, *Rise of Biblical Criticism.*

25. The best comprehensive study of Transcendentalism is Philip F. Gura, *American Transcendentalism: A History* (New York: Hill and Wang, 2007), but also see Barbara L. Packer, *The Transcendentalists* (Athens: University of Georgia Press, 2007), and Octavius Brooks Frothingham, *Transcendentalism in New England* (1876; repr., Philadelphia: University of Pennsylvania Press, 2016).

26. James Elliot Cabot, *A Memoir of Ralph Waldo Emerson*, 2 vols. (Boston: Houghton Mifflin, 1887), 1:249; Caroline Healy Dall, *Transcendentalism in New England: A Lecture* (Boston: Sold by Roberts Brothers, 1897), 16; and R. W. Emerson, W. H. Channing, and J. F. Clarke, eds., *Memoirs of Margaret Fuller Ossoli*, 2 vols. (Boston: Phillips, Sampson, 1852), 2:5.

27. Charles Mayo Ellis, *An Essay on Transcendentalism* (Boston: Crocker and Ruggles, 1842), 11, 19.

28. Ibid., 23–24, 72.

29. *The Journals and Miscellaneous Notebooks of Ralph Waldo Emerson*, ed. William H. Gilman et al. 16 vols. (Cambridge: Harvard University Press, 1960–1982), 3:78; Emerson, "The Miracle of Our Being," in Arthur Cushman McGiffert, ed., *Young Emerson Speaks: Unpublished Discourses on Many Subjects* (Boston: Houghton Mifflin, 1938), 210.

30. Emerson, *Journals and Miscellaneous Notebooks*, 2:284.

31. Ibid., 4:200.

32. Ibid., 4:109–122.

33. Ibid., 4:222–23, 225.

34. Ibid., 3:190.

35. Cabot, *Memoir of Ralph Waldo Emerson*, 1:259.

36. This was Emerson's second publication, following by a year a *Historical Discourse* delivered at the bicentennial of his hometown, Concord, Massachusetts.

37. Emerson to William Emerson, September 29, 1826, in *Letters*, 1:176. Reed's book was *Observations on the Growth of the Mind* (1826).

38. Patrick W. Carey, ed., *The Early Works of Orestes A. Brownson*, 5 vols. (Milwaukee, Wis.: Marquette University Press, 2000–), 3:376; Elizabeth Peabody, *United States Magazine and Democratic Review* 1 (February 1838): 319; Francis Bowen, review of Emerson's *Nature*, *Christian Examiner* 21 (January 1837): 377.

39. Emerson to Thomas Carlyle, September 17, 1836, in Joseph Slater, ed., *The Correspondence of Emerson and Carlyle* (New York: Columbia University Press, 1964), 149.

40. Emerson, *Nature*, in *Essays and Lectures*, 10.

41. Ibid., 7, 47, 49.

42. On Brownson's life, see Patrick W. Carey, *Orestes A. Brownson: American Religious Weathervane* (Grand Rapids, Mich.: W. B. Eerdman's, 2004).

43. On such early labor movements, see Sean Wilentz, *Chants Democratic: New York City and the Rise of the American Working Class, 1788–1850* (New York: Oxford University Press, 1984).

44. Orestes Brownson, *New Views of Christianity, Society, and the Church* (Boston: J. Munroe, 1836), 91–94.

45. On Ripley, see Charles Crowe, *George Ripley: Transcendentalist and Utopian Socialist* (Athens: University of Georgia Press, 1967); and O. B. Frothingham, *George Ripley* (Boston: Houghton Mifflin, 1882).

46. On Brook Farm, see Sterling Delano, *Brook Farm: The Dark Side of Utopia* (Cambridge: Harvard University Press, 2004).

47. Orestes Brownson, *The Convert* (1857), in *The Works of Orestes A. Brownson*, collected and arranged by Henry F. Brownson, 20 vols. (Detroit, Mich.: T. Nourse, 1882–1907), 5:82–83.

48. Emerson, "New England Reformers," in *Essays and Lectures*, 596, 598.

49. Ibid., 599.

50. Emerson, *Journals and Miscellaneous Notebooks*, 4:207–8, 356–57.

51. Emerson, "The Divinity School Address," in *Essays and Lectures*, 84–85.

52. Ibid., 80.

53. Margaret Fuller, "Emerson's Essays," in *Life Without and Life Within*, ed. Arthur B. Fuller (Boston: Brown, Taggard and Chase, 1860), 194.

54. Emerson, "Self-Reliance," in Fuller, ed., *Life Without*, 259, 261, 260.

55. Ibid., 275, 282.

56. Emerson, *Journals and Miscellaneous Notebooks*, 7:342.

57. Emerson, "The Over-Soul," in *Essays and Lectures*, 385–86; 392.

58. Emerson, "Compensation," in *Essays and Lectures*, 301.

59. Dolores Bird Carpenter, ed., *The Selected Letters of Lidian Jackson Emerson* (Columbia: University of Missouri Press, 1987), 89; Emerson, *Journals and Miscellaneous Notebooks*, 11:53.

60. Emerson, "Experience," in *Essays and Lectures*, 471, 473.

61. Ibid., 478, 487.

62. See Daniel Walker Howe's magisterial *What Hath God Wrought: The Transformation of America, 1815–1848* (New York: Oxford University Press, 2007) for an overview of this period of American history.

63. Emerson, "Experience," in *Essays and Lectures*, 491–92.

64. Emerson, "Politics," in *Essays and Lectures*, 559.

65. Ibid., 564–65, 567.

66. Ralph Waldo Emerson, "An Address . . . on . . . the Emancipation of the Negroes in the West Indies," in *Emerson's Antislavery Writings*, ed. Len Gougeon and Joel Myerson (New Haven, Conn.: Yale University Press, 1995), 20, 32.

67. See *Emerson's Antislavery Writings*, 39–91.

68. Ralph Waldo Emerson, "Address to the Citizens of Concord," in *Emerson's Antislavery Writings*, 53, 65–66; Emerson, *Journals and Miscellaneous Notebooks*, 11:346.

69. Emerson, "Fate," in *Essays and Lectures*, 943, 945, 949, 953.

70. For a convincing discussion of this transformation of Emerson's vision, see David M. Robinson, *Emerson and the Conduct of Life: Pragmatism and Ethical Purpose in the Later Work* (New York: Cambridge University Press, 1993).

71. Emerson, *Journals and Miscellaneous Notebooks*, 15:405.

72. Ralph Waldo Emerson, "American Civilization," *Atlantic Monthly* 9 (April 1862): 509.

73. Emerson, "The President's Proclamation," in *Emerson's Antislavery Writings*, 131.

74. Emerson, "The Fortune of the Republic," in *Complete Works of Ralph*

Waldo Emerson, 14 vols. (Boston: Houghton Mifflin, 1883), 11:399. Also see the version in *Emerson's Antislavery Writings*, 137–54.

75. Emerson, *Complete Works*, 11:402–3.

76. Ibid., 11:404.

77. Ibid., 11:406–7, 413.

78. Ibid., 11:419.

79. Ibid., 11:399.

80. Ibid., 11:418, 421.

81. Mickiewicz quoted by Ludwik Krzyzanowiski, "Mickiewicz and Emerson," in *Adam Mickiewicz: Poet of Poland*, ed. Manfred Kridl (New York: Columbia University Press, 1951), 267.

82. Reported by Lidian Emerson to her husband, June 10, 1848, in *The Selected Letters of Lidian Jackson Emerson*, ed. Dolores Bird Carpenter (Columbia: University of Missouri Press, 1987), 157.

83. Philarète Chasles, *Anglo-American Literature and Manners* (New York: Scribner, 1852), 192.

84. See *English Review* 12 (London: Rivington, 1849); reprinted in New York's *Littel's Living Age* 24 (November 1849): 344–56.

85. David W. Blight, *Frederick Douglass: Prophet of Freedom* (New York: Simon and Schuster, 2018), 470.

86. Theodore S. Wright, Charles B. Wary, and James McCune Smith, *An Address to Three Thousand Colored Citizens of New-York* (New York, 1846), 15; James Monroe Whitefield in Joan R. Sherman, *Invisible Poets: Afro-Americans of the Nineteenth Century* (Urbana: University of Illinois Press, 1974), 49.

87. Margaret Fuller, *Woman in the Nineteenth Century* (1845; repr., New York: W. W. Norton, 1971), 37.

88. This is widely attributed to Carnegie but evidently does not appear in any of his works. For a very similar sentiment see Ella Wheeler Wilcox, "Let the Past Go," in *The Heart of the New Thought* (Chicago: Psychic Research Company, 1902), 7.

89. See James Bradley Thayer, *A Western Journey with Mr. Emerson* (Boston: Osgood, 1884); John Muir, *Our National Parks* (Boston: Houghton Mifflin, 1901), 135; and James Perrin Wilson, *John Burroughs and the Place of Nature* (Athens: University of Georgia Press, 2006), chap. 1.

90. Alexis de Tocqueville, *Democracy in America* (Chicago: University of Chicago Press, 2000), 482–84.

91. On such misappropriation of Emerson, see, for example, George Kateb, *The Inner Ocean: Individualism and Democratic Culture* (Ithaca, N.Y.: Cornell University Press, 1992).

Chapter 3. William James: The Active Life

1. On Henry James Sr., see Alfred Habegger, *The Father: A Life of Henry James Sr.* (New York: Farrar, Straus, and Giroux, 1984).

2. Ralph Waldo Emerson to Lidian Emerson, March 10 and 11, 1842, in *The Letters of Ralph Waldo Emerson*, ed. Ralph L. Rusk, 6 vols. (New York: Columbia University Press, 1939), 3:26; James Russell Lowell in *New York Times*, September 2, 1910.

3. The best recent biography of William James is Robert D. Richardson Jr., *William James: In the Maelstrom of American Modernism* (Boston: Houghton Mifflin, 2006); but see also R. W. B. Lewis, *The Jameses: A Family Narrative* (New York: Farrar, Straus, and Giroux, 1991); Gay Wilson Allen, *William James: A Biography* (New York: Viking Press, 1967); and Howard M. Feinstein, *Becoming William James* (Ithaca, N.Y.: Cornell University Press, 1984). A nice recent assessment of James's significance is Amy Kittelstrom, *The Religion of Democracy: Seven Liberals and the American Moral Tradition* (New York: Penguin Press, 2015), 155–210.

4. Henry James Sr., "Emerson," *Atlantic Monthly* 94 (1904): 740. James wrote this around 1868 and delivered it to some audiences. After Emerson's death, William James published it.

5. Henry James Sr. to Emerson, October 3, 1843, cited in Habegger, *The Father*, 202.

6. Henry James Sr. to Emerson, May 11, 1843, cited in Habegger, *The Father*, 202.

7. *Correspondence of William James*, 12 vols. (Charlottesville: University of Virginia Press, 1992–2004), 1:289.

8. Fragment of letter from Henry James Sr., probably to Christopher Cranch, cited in Habegger, *The Father*, 430.

9. See Randall Fuller, *The Book That Changed America: How Darwin's Theory of Evolution Ignited a Nation* (New York: Viking, 2017).

10. See Paul Jerome Croce, *Science and Religion in the Era of William James* (Chapel Hill: University of North Carolina Press, 1995), 87–148, for

a good discussion of Darwin's influence at this point in James's life, and as well Croce's more recent *Young William James Thinking* (Baltimore, Md.: Johns Hopkins University Press, 2018), 69–75.

11. James to Henry James Sr., September 5, 1867, in *Correspondence of William James*, 4:194.

12. See E. Brook Holifield, *Theology in America: Christian Thought from the Age of the Puritans to the Civil War* (New Haven, Conn.: Yale University Press, 2003), 372–89.

13. See James John Garth Wilkinson, *Emanuel Swedenborg: A Biography* (London: William Newbery, 1849). Henry James Sr. named one of his sons Garth after the author of this biography.

14. See John S. Haller Jr., *Swedenborg, Mesmer, and the Mind/Body Connection* (West Chester, Pa.: The Swedenborg Foundation, 2010).

15. [Henry James Sr.], *Tracts for the New Times, No. 1: Letter to a Swedenborgian* (New York: John Allen, 1847), 20–21.

16. Henry James Sr., *Christianity: The Logic of Creation* (New York: D. Appleton, 1857), 68; and *The Nature of Evil* (New York: D. Appleton, 1855), 77.

17. *Correspondence of William James*, 4:221.

18. Ibid.

19. Ibid., 4:255.

20. William Dean Howells, review of Henry James Sr.'s *The Secret of Swedenborg*, *Atlantic Monthly* 24 (July 1869): 762–63; Charles Sanders Peirce, "James's Secret of Swedenborg," *North American Review* 110 (April 1870), reprinted in *Writings of Charles S. Peirce*, 8 vols. (Bloomington: Indiana University Press, 1982–2010), 2:437; *Correspondence of William James*, 1:102.

21. Richardson, *William James*, 96.

22. William James, "Diary," February 1, 1870, in Richardson, *William James*, 111.

23. Ibid., March 22, 1870, in Richardson, *William James*, 112–13.

24. William James, *The Varieties of Religious Experience* (Cambridge: Harvard University Press, 1985), 134.

25. *Correspondence of William James*, 10:619.

26. See Louis Menand, *The Metaphysical Club* (New York: Farrar, Straus, and Giroux, 2001).

27. Emerson, "The Natural History of Intellect," in Emerson, *Complete Works*, 12:4.

28. Ibid., 12:15–16.

29. William James, "Rationality, Activity, Faith," *Princeton Review*, 4th ser., 10 (July 1882): 68.

30. William James, *Essays in Philosophy* (Cambridge: Harvard University Press, 1978), 18.

31. Ibid., 21.

32. William James, *Manuscript Lectures* (Cambridge: Harvard University Press, 1988), 23.

33. Ibid.

34. Ibid., 30.

35. James, "Rationality, Activity, Faith," 65–66.

36. Ibid., 73–74,86. On the subject of James's understanding of the relationship between science and faith, see David Hollinger's "'Damned for God's Glory': William James and the Scientific Vindication of Protestant Culture," in Wayne Proudfoot, ed., *William James and a Science of Religions: Reexperiencing the Varieties of Religious Experience* (New York: Columbia University Press, 2004), 9–30.

37. Henry James, February 3, 1882, *Complete Letters of Henry James*, 4 vols. (Lincoln: University of Nebraska Press, 2008–), 2:376.

38. F. O. Matthiessen, *The James Family* (New York: Knopf, 1961), 447–48.

39. *Correspondence of William James*, 5:227–28.

40. Ibid., 1:344.

41. William James, *Essays in Psychology* (Cambridge: Harvard University Press, 1983), 143–44.

42. Ibid., 154.

43. Emerson, "Natural History of Intellect," 12:15.

44. William James, *The Principles of Psychology*, 3 vols. (Cambridge: Harvard University Press, 1981), 1:180–81.

45. Ibid., 1:182. Jonathan Edwards, *Freedom of the Will*, in *The Works of Jonathan Edwards*, 26 vols. (New Haven, Conn.: Yale University Press, 1957–2008), 1:143.

46. *Correspondence of William James*, 6:510, 2:200.

47. William James, *The Will to Believe* (Cambridge: Harvard University Press, 1979), 48, 52, 53, 55.

48. Ibid., 55.

49. Ibid., 13–15.

50. Ibid., 29–30.

51. See Hollinger, "'Damned for God's Glory,'" for a discussion of James's long-standing struggle to reconcile faith with science.

52. *Correspondence of William James*, 8:155.

53. Ibid., 8:390–91.

54. Eve of the Christian feast day of English Saint Walpurga, an eighth-century abbess who traveled to Germany as a missionary, that was celebrated throughout Europe with bonfires and dancing. Christians prayed to this saint to protect themselves from witchcraft; hence, the bonfires. She reportedly brought in many converts from the heathenism that reigned in central Europe.

55. *Correspondence of William James*, 8:390.

56. Henry David Thoreau, *The Maine Woods* (Princeton, N.J.: Princeton University Press, 1972), 70–71.

57. See the essays in Proudfoot, ed., *William James and a Science of Religions* for a good sense of the background to the lectures and their larger significance in both religious studies and the development of James's pragmatism; and David C. Lamberth, *William James and the Metaphysics of Experience* (New York: Cambridge University Press, 199), 97–145.

58. *Correspondence of William James*, 8:439.

59. William James, *Talks to Teachers on Psychology* (Cambridge: Harvard University Press, 1983), 4.

60. See Wayne Proudfoot, "Pragmatism and 'an Unseen Order' in Varieties," in Proudfoot, ed., *William James and a Science of Religions*, 31–47.

61. James, *Varieties of Religious Experience*, 150, 25–26; also see the essays in Proudfoot, ed., *William James and a Science of Religions*, particularly Hollinger's "'Damned for God's Glory'" (9–30).

62. James, *Varieties of Religious Experience*, 46.

63. Ibid., 112, 120.

64. Ibid., 161–62, 139.

65. Ibid., 220.

66. Ibid., 254, 292.

67. Ibid., 303.

68. Ibid., 338.

69. Ibid., 408, 414.

70. Charles Sanders Peirce, "Pragmatism," in *Collected Papers of Charles*

Sanders Peirce, ed. Charles Hartshorne and Paul Weiss, 6 vols. (Cambridge: Harvard University Press, 1960–1966), vol. 5, section 12.

71. Henry James to Charles Eliot Norton, February 4, 1872, in James, *Letters*, 1:269.

72. On Peirce see Joseph Brent, *Charles Sanders Peirce: A Life*, rev. and enlarged ed. (Bloomington: Indiana University Press, 1998).

73. In a letter of Edward Youmans, in which he records a visit with W. K. Clifford, who gave the assessment, in John Fiske, *Edward Livingstone Youmans* (New York: Appleton's, 1894), 340.

74. James to Henry James, March 14, 1875, cited in Brent, *Charles Sanders Peirce*, 103.

75. See James's description of the history of this idea in his *Pragmatism* (1907).

76. Peirce, "Pragmatism Made Easy," MS cited in Menand, *Metaphysical Club*, 226.

77. Peirce, "How to Make Our Ideas Clear," in *Writings of Charles Sanders Peirce*, 8 vols. (Bloomington: Indiana University Press, 1982), 3:273.

78. Peirce, "Fraser's *The Work of George Berkeley*," in *Writings of Charles Sanders Peirce*, 3:282.

79. Ibid., 3:284.

80. William James, *Essays in Religion and Morality* (Cambridge: Harvard University Press, 1982), 112.

81. William James, *Pragmatism* (Cambridge: Harvard University Press, 1975), 138, 141–42.

82. Ibid., 11–15.

83. James had first announced the term "pragmatism" in a lecture, "Philosophical Conceptions and Practical Results," at the University of California Berkeley, August 26, 1898.

84. James, *Pragmatism*, 31.

85. Ibid., 104.

86. Ralph Barton Perry, *The Thought and Character of William James*, 2 vols. (Boston: Little, Brown, 1935), 2:315.

87. James, *Pragmatism*, 138.

88. *Correspondence of William James*, 3:344.

89. William James, "Robert Gould Shaw," in *Essays in Religion and Morality*, (Cambridge, Mass.: Harvard University Press, 1982), 72–73.

90. On James's anti-imperialistic stance, see Alexander Livingston, *Damn Great Empire! William James and the Politics of Pragmatism* (New York: Oxford University Press, 2016); and George Cotkin, *William James, Public Philosopher* (Baltimore, Md.: Johns Hopkins University Press, 1990), 123–51.

91. William James, *Essays, Comments, Reviews* (Cambridge: Harvard University Press, 1987), 156–57.

92. George Santayana, "The Genteel Tradition," in *Selected Critical Writings of George Santayana*, 2 vols. (London: Cambridge University Press, 1968), 1:99.

93. *Correspondence of William James*, 11:267.

94. Ibid., 12:18–19.

95. William James to Maxwell J. Savage, January 4, 1910, in Frederick Scott, ed., *William James: Selected Correspondence* (Columbus: Ohio State University Press, 1986), 534.

96. See Gail Thain Parker, *Mind Cure in New England: From the Civil War to World War I* (Hanover, N.H.: University Press of New England, 1973), for a good discussion of this topic among Emerson and his successors.

97. William James, *A Pluralistic Universe* (Cambridge: Harvard University Press, 1977), 70–71.

98. Ibid., 143–44.

99. See Joshua I. Miller, *Democratic Temperament: The Legacy of William James* (Lawrence: University of Kansas Press, 1997), for a good discussion of James's significance in American culture.

100. W. E. B. Du Bois, in *The Education of Black People: Ten Critiques, 1906–1960*, ed. Herbert Aptheker (Amherst: University of Massachusetts Press, 1973), 89. Bruce Kuklick, who in his *Churchmen and Philosophers: From Jonathan Edwards to John Dewey* (New Haven, Conn.: Yale University Press, 1985) summarizes two centuries of American religious and philosophical thought, ends his study not with James but Dewey, whom he sees as the premier exponent of pragmatism in the public sphere.

101. Josiah Royce, "William James and the Philosophy of Life," in *William James and Other Essays* (New York: Macmillan, 1911), 10.

102. Santayana, "Genteel Tradition," 99.

Chapter 4. John Rawls: The Search for Twentieth-Century Justice

1. James first used this phrase in *The Varieties of Religious Experience* (Cambridge: Harvard University Press, 1985), 292.

2. *Harvard Crimson*, April 27, 1966. Also see Katrina Forrester, *In the Shadow of Justice: Postwar Liberalism and the Remaking of Political Philosophy* (Princeton, N.J.: Princeton University Press, 2019), 50–53.

3. The following account is drawn from Lawrence E. Eichel et al., *The Harvard Strike* (Boston: Houghton Mifflin, 1970), and my own account in manuscript journals now deposited in the Harvard Archives at the Houghton Library, Harvard University.

4. See Forrester, *In the Shadow of Justice*, 56–71.

5. A good biographical account is Thomas Pogge, *John Rawls: His Life and Theory of Justice*, trans. Michelle Kosch (New York: Oxford University Press, 2007); but see also Percy B. Lehning, *John Rawls: An Introduction* (2006; repr., Cambridge: Cambridge University Press, 2009), 1–16. Also helpful in this section were Pogge, *Realizing Rawls* (Ithaca, N.Y.: Cornell University Press, 1989) and, most recently, Andrius Gališanka, *John Rawls: The Path to a Theory of Justice* (Cambridge: Harvard University Press, 2019).

6. John Rawls, "On My Religion," in Rawls, *A Brief Inquiry into the Meaning of Sin and Faith, with "On My Religion,"* ed. Thomas Nagel (Cambridge: Harvard University Press, 2009), 261–69.

7. Ibid.

8. See P. Mackenzie Bok, "To the Mountaintop Again: The Early Rawls and Post-Protestant Ethics in Postwar America," *Modern Intellectual History* 14, no. 1 (April 2017): 153–85, for a compelling discussion of the significance of his Princeton years on Rawls's *Theory of Justice*, particularly the importance of his teachers. Also see Gališanka, *John Rawls*, 17–44.

9. Rawls, *A Brief Inquiry*, 244.

10. See Pogge, *John Rawls*, 13.

11. Ibid., 14.

12. See Bok, "To the Mountaintop," on Rawls's work in ethics. Rawls

took Black's seminar while he was a visiting graduate student at Cornell but still technically enrolled at Princeton.

13. See Gališanka, *John Rawls*, 97–101; and Stephen Toulmin, *An Examination of the Place of Reason in Ethics* (Cambridge: Cambridge University Press, 1950).

14. John von Neumann and Oskar Morgenstern, *Theory of Games and Economic Behavior* (Princeton, N.J.: Princeton University Press, 1944).

15. See Gališanka, *John Rawls*, 151–59.

16. John Rawls, *A Theory of Justice*, rev. ed. (1971; repr., Cambridge: Harvard University Press, 1999), 24, 513, 17.

17. Ibid., 28.

18. Ibid., 7, 11.

19. Gališanka, *John Rawls*, offers a detailed look at the evolution of Rawls's thought during this seminal period.

20. Rawls, *A Theory of Justice*, 3, 25.

21. Ibid., 11, 17–18.

22. Ibid., 18–19.

23. Ibid., 53.

24. Ibid.

25. Ibid., 7.

26. Ibid., 172–74.

27. Ibid., 192–93.

28. Ibid., 244–45.

29. Forrester, *In the Shadow of Justice*, 72–103, has a cogent discussion of this issue with regard to conscientious objection.

30. Rawls, *A Theory of Justice*, 314.

31. Ibid., 386.

32. Ibid., 468–74.

33. John Rawls, *Political Liberalism*, expanded edition (1993; repr., New York: Columbia University Press, 2005).

34. Ibid., 215–20.

35. Ibid., 139.

36. John Rawls, *The Law of Peoples* (Cambridge: Harvard University Press, 1999).

37. Robert Nozick, *Anarchy, State, and Utopia* (New York: Basic Books, 1974). See also Forrester, *In the Shadow of Justice*, especially 127–32.

38. Michael J. Sandel, *Liberalism and the Limits of Justice* (New York: Cambridge University Press, 1982). See also Forrester, *In the Shadow of Justice*, 255–58.

39. Michael Walzer, *Spheres of Justice: A Defense of Pluralism and Equality* (New York: Basic Books, 1983). See also Forrester, *In the Shadow of Justice*, 53–59, 99–101.

Coda

1. Robert Cushman, "Reasons and Considerations Touching the Lawfulness of Removing out of England into the Parts of America," in Dwight B. Heath, ed., *A Journal of the Pilgrims at Plymouth* (1622; repr., New York: Corinth Books, 1969), 94–95.

2. John Winthrop, "A Modell of Christian Charitie," 92. The full text of Winthrop's sermon is in Edmund S. Morgan, ed., *Puritan Political Ideas* (Indianapolis, Ind.: Bobbs-Merrill, 1965), 76–93.

3. Thomas Hooker, *The Danger of Desertion, a Farewell Sermon* (London: G. M. for George Edwards, 1641), 6–7, 5. Hooker delivered it in the early 1630s.

4. Winthrop, "A Modell of Christian Charitie," 92–93. Also see Daniel T. Rodgers, *As a City on a Hill: The Story of America's Most Famous Lay Sermon* (Princeton, N.J.: Princeton University Press, 2018).

5. Henry David Thoreau, *Walden* (1854; repr., Princeton, N.J.: Princeton University Press, 1971), 53.

Index